Has your faith become a chore where once it was a passion?
Are you tired of the self-serving mentality of our culture?
Do you long to move deeper in authentic spirituality?

"Come follow me ..."
(Jesus)

Everything is different. Nothing has changed. In contemporary culture, Christ's call to costly discipleship is still the key to life itself. In this book, author Pete Greig chronicles his own pilgrimage from "The Vision" to the discovery of *The Vow*—an ancient oath of deep friendship in allegiance to Jesus.

If you're ready for such a commitment—a cause to live and die for—join an underground movement around the world as they take this vow. A change is coming, and this is your invitation.

THE AUTHOR

Pete Greig is the founder of 24-7 Prayer—an international, interdenominational community committed to prayer, mission, and justice. Based in England, Greig currently lives in Kansas City, Mo., where he is an active member of a missional community. Greig is recognized as an adviser and teacher in many countries, has authored three books, and has contributed to numerous programs on television and radio. He and his wife Samie have two young children.

the Vision and the Vow

RE-DISCOVERING LIFE AND GRACE

PETE GREIG

[RELEVANTBOOKS]

"Come follow me ..."
(Jesus)

Published by Relevant Books
A division of Relevant Media Group, Inc.

www.relevant-books.com
www.relevantmediagroup.com

© 2004 Peter Greig

Published by arrangement with Kingsway Publications, Eastbourne, England

Design by Relevant Solutions
www.relevant-solutions.com
Cover, Illustrations and interior design by Joshua Smith
Contributing Illustrator: Julie West

Relevant Books is a registered trademark of Relevant Media Group, Inc., and is registered in the U.S. Patent and Trademark Office.

For information or bulk orders:
RELEVANT MEDIA GROUP, INC.
POST OFFICE BOX 951127
LAKE MARY, FL 32795
407-333-7152

International Standard Book Number: 0-9729276-2-X
02 03 04 05 9 8 7 6 5 4 3 2

Printed in the United States of America

Vow (vou): n. A promise made to God. The promise is binding,
and so differs from a simple resolution, which is a present purpose to do
or omit certain things in the future ... A vow is an act of generosity towards God.
(The Catholic Encyclopedia)

DEDICATED TO:
Gill Greig-Allen, who planted three mustard seeds in very good soil.

WITH THANKS TO:
The many people who have given themselves to this project. Especially: Samie, Hudson, and Daniel, Phil (Tin Tin) Anderson, Markus Lägel, Phil Togwell, Dr. Pete Ward, Justin Blake, Tim (Kingshot) Harrold, Carla Trundle, Phil Baldwin, Stez, Gill and Peter Greig-Allen, Ken Costa, Floyd McClung, Jason Mandryk, Greg Russinger, Richard Herkes and all at Kingsway, Cara Davis and all at RELEVANT, Dave Roberts, our "visionaries" from every walk of life who commented on their favorite lines, the 24-7 crew around the world, and all the guys who read the first manuscript of this book (which no longer exists).

xi

COVENANT
"SACRIFICE FUELS THE FIRE"

GENESIS
"CONSPIRACY IS BREATHING ONCE AGAIN"

CHAPTER NONE
'TIS BUT A VISION

"When God wants to initiate a new movement in history,
he does not intervene directly, but sends us dreams and visions that can, if
attended to, initiate the process." —Walter Wink[1]

A couple of hundred weeks ago, I wrote a load of words on a wall with a marker. I can't be sure exactly how many weeks ago it was because I never inscribed the date in my diary; at the time, I had no idea that what I was writing would touch a lot of people, and I certainly never dreamed that I would be here now, pecking away at a keyboard with my index finger, trying to write a book about what happened next.

If I'd known, I guess I would have used my best handwriting and taken a commemorative photo. Actually, if I'd known the way "The Vision" would spread to touch more than a million lives, I would have expressed a few things differently, been a bit less gung-ho (I'd drunk a lot of coffee), and been a bit more humorous. In fact, if I'd known what would happen next, I might even have taught myself to type.

But then again, if I'd known these things back then, I'd almost certainly have "seized-up"—my marker meaningfully poised, frozen like a rabbit in the headlights or a kid in the spotlights of his first school play.

But back then, it was just me and God and a cup of coffee in a room in the

---

1. Walter Wink, *Engaging the Powers: Discernment and Resistance in a World of Domination* (Augsburg Fortress, Minneapolis, MN: 1992) p. 285.

middle of the night trying to make sense of some things, trying to scrape some words from the back of my mind onto paper.

And the two hundred weeks since that night have been quite a ride, with highs and lows like you wouldn't believe. It's been the valley of the shadow and the view from the top of the mountain, up and down, again and again, all in a couple of hundred weeks. For some of the places I have walked, there is simply no vocabulary.

THE GOOD STUFF

First, there's been the explosion: Two hundred weeks ago, I had no idea that the simple, single, scruffy prayer room in which I was standing was preparing to multiply itself all around the world. At the time of writing, it's manifested itself in no fewer than fifty-four nations, and we've been praying continually ever since.

This unexpected wave of prayer has enabled many of us to take up surfing. The bewildered kid with the marker has found himself preaching all over the world: in a jazz club in Stockholm, a cinema in Kansas City, and from the ancient pulpit of an English cathedral. Yesterday I even preached on an ocean-liner!

Finding myself in such places, I do my best to impersonate an adult.

And while all of this has been happening, these two hundred weeks have been the catalyst for friendships of a lifetime. I've had maybe a thousand meetings— mainly in coffee shops and bars drinking double-shot lattes (fairly-traded beans wherever possible), or orange juice when my vitamin count feels as low as my sleep quota. There've also been tears, frustration, and the arrival of a few gray hairs (which actually really help with the whole pretending-to-be-an-adult thing).

THE BAD STUFF

There really is no subtle way to tell you what happened, so I'll just come out and say it starkly: About one hundred and fifty weeks ago, my wife nearly died of a brain tumor. The size of an orange, we were told. Suddenly things that had seemed important disappeared off the radar without a trace. Finding ourselves set down in the valley of the shadow of death, God's book and God's people comforted us more than we ever knew they could. But we were terrified, and in my turmoil, I felt a million miles from that kid with the marker, so intent on saving the planet. I couldn't even save my own wife.

During those weeks, as Samie somehow came through surgery successfully and began to try to rebuild her life with the reality of uncontrollable epilepsy (pretty name for such an ugly thing), I found myself as the primary caregiver for our kids. Without doubt, the greatest joy of these two hundred weeks has been watching our two sons grow from babies into hilarious little people. There's a way they laugh when I tickle them, and a shape their mouths make when they yawn …

And so, the wannabe revolutionary found himself changing diapers, discussing the Teletubbies, and warming bottles of milk in the night. But this season of frontline caring turned out to be the most wonderful gift of intimacy, the kindest hijacking in history, and looking back, I wouldn't have missed it for anything. How many dads get to nurse their kids through chicken pox and watch them play the way I did each day?

A couple of hundred weeks on from that first prayer room, one hundred and fifty from Samie's surgery, she's alive by the sheer grace of God; we're alive, and we celebrate birthdays—each new candle on the cake—like you wouldn't believe! Admittedly, we often feel bruised and beaten, "frayed and nibbled survivors in a fallen world,"[2] but we also feel privileged to be alive, more determined than ever to make our days count for eternity.

So, life's been kind of crazy by anyone's standards since that piece of late-night graffiti. And of course I have changed. I am no longer the guy with the marker; I guess I'm more beat-up. These days I feel more gangly than gung-ho, more broken and bewildered, less certain, more in love with my wife, with life, than I can

---

2. Annie Dillard, *Pilgrim at Tinker Creek* (HarperCollins Publishers, New York, NY: 1998) p. 245.

possibly say, dependent on God like a fistful of dust plugged into life-support.

VISION TRUE

So I look at the stranger writing those words on a wall a couple of hundred weeks ago, and I take him a little less seriously than perhaps I should. But then again, as I read what he's writing, something in me still stirs—a latent longing to live like that for Jesus, for a generation, for a cause. So perhaps nothing has changed at all.

And ironically, while I feel weaker and further from the dream of that night, the fact is that there are now networks of people praying all over the world, missional communities emerging, and worldviews being shaped. So perhaps we are actually closer now than we ever were to that "army of young people" I envisioned as I wrote the words on the wall that night. Perhaps I have staggered and stumbled against every animal instinct into the truth that God is strong when I am not, and that the kingdom of heaven is populated not by those who've "got it all together," but rather by the muttering meek—disoriented pilgrims, the dazed and confused who mourn.

George MacDonald, the nineteenth century Scottish mystic who inspired J.R.R. Tolkien and C.S. Lewis, compares the Christian vision to a beautiful portrait painted by God, depicting the person we will one day become:

> *"'Tis but a vision, Lord; I do not mean*
> *That thus I am, or have one moment been—*
> *'Tis but a picture hung upon my wall*
> *To measure dull contentment therewithal,*
> *And know behind the human how I fall;*
> *A vision true, of what one day shall be*
> *When thou hast had thy very will with me."*
> *(The Diary of an Old Soul[3])*

---

3. George MacDonald, *The Diary of an Old Soul*, first published in 1880, this edition: SPCK: 2001.

To those who accuse "The Vision" of being idealistic, I can think of no better response than George McDonald's poem. I would be a liar if I pretended that light currently "flickers from every secret motive" in my heart. "Sulphuric tears" scorch my prayer life less than I would like. Sometimes—more often than I want you to know—I fly on autopilot, praying as if it all depends merely on me, yet living lazily as if it all depends on God. George MacDonald was right. You hold in your hand little more than a dream, "a picture hung upon my wall" measuring my own "dull contentment," and yet it is also a "vision true" anticipating "what one day shall be."

People tend to have portraits painted or photographed when they are in their prime, as a flattering reminder of the fading beauty that was. But the passing years are not cruel for us in Christ. Quite the reverse! The Word of God assures us that our features "gradually become brighter and more beautiful as God enters our lives and we become like him" (2 Corinthians 3:18 MSG).

So here we all are, a couple of hundred weeks down the road, and I'm pecking away at a keyboard looking for words with which to explore, expound, and expand on the ones I wrote so carelessly on that wall with a marker, and I'm hoping that somehow I might help you fall a little more in love with Jesus.

And if meetings in Starbucks and words on a page really can do that, then count me in. I'm two hundred weeks more certain that nothing on earth matters more than this single thing: that we might see Jesus as He truly is, hear His call to follow come what may, and love Him back, "dangerously, obsessively, and undeniably."

THE CALL TO DISCIPLESHIP

In its opening stanza, we are reminded that "The Vision," quite simply, "is Jesus," and the poem ends with a glimpse of His triumphant return as "the original dreamer, the ultimate winner. Guaranteed." The Lord Jesus Christ is the beginning and ending of the Christian vision. In fact, He is the beginning and ending of all things. How then should we respond to His company on the journey of our lives? According to the Gospels, Jesus has always invited people to relate to Him in three ways:

- To know Him as Friend.
- To trust Him as Savior.
- To obey Him as Lord.[4]

The invitation to friendship and salvation rings out from pulpits and products loud and clear around the Western world, but Christ's incontrovertible call to costly commitment and sacrificial obedience sometimes seems to have been removed from the canon of grace altogether.

Two thousand years ago, Christ's simple invitation to "come follow me" echoed around the shores of Galilee, and the words I wrote on a wall some two hundred weeks ago add nothing whatsoever to that original, revolutionary call to Christian discipleship. Those first followers simply saw something in Jesus that day for which they were willing to lay down everything, and they appear to have done it impulsively and joyfully. They didn't know then that their choices would be recorded in scripture, nor were they aware of the pain that awaited them on their journey. But they saw something in Jesus of Nazareth that made them want to follow Him sacrificially and to learn from Him, more than they wanted anything else on earth. They caught a vision—a dangerous, obsessive, and wonderful epiphany that has captivated hearts ever since.

Even now, this Galilean calls us by name to leave our nets, abandon small dreams of token empires, and follow Him into the great unknown. His vision

4. John R. Scott, *Christian Basics: An Invitation to Discipleship* (Baker Book House, Grand Rapids, MI: 2003) pp. 15-17.

for our lives is a treasure worth everything we own—worth living for and dying for. It's the vision for which we were born: created by God as a gift of love to His broken, beautiful world.

In our
day heaven and earth
are on tiptoe waiting for the
emerging of a Spirit-led, Spirit-
empowered people. All of creation
watches expectantly for the springing
up of a disciplined, freely gathered,
martyr people who know in this life
the life and power of the kingdom
of God. It has happened
before. It can happen
again ...
(Richard Foster[5])

5. Richard Foster, *Celebration of Discipline* (Harper & Row, San Francisco, CA: 1978) p. 150.

VISION

REVELATION
THE DREAM OF GOD

"this is the longing of creation itself,
the groaning of the Spirit,
the very dream of God ..."

"Let us fix our eyes on Jesus, the author and perfecter of our faith, who for the
joy set before him endured the cross ..."
(Hebrews 12:2)

CHAPTER ONE
LIVING WITH VISION (IN A CYNICAL AGE)

BRRMMPH.

SP-LOSH.

Adrian's yellow pedalo hit mine at ninety degrees, followed by a great arc of green lake water drenching me in one go.

BOOPH.

Another pedalo came in from behind, and thus began one of the lesser-known naval battles of our time.

If you've ever actually been out in a pedalo boat, you may understand: They always seem like such a great idea until you find yourself afloat and realize that in fact, you have sentenced yourself to thirty minutes in purgatory, half an hour pedaling a primary-colored plastic toy very slowly around in a few feet of water, maniacally determined to "Have Fun With Friends."

And so, with tedious predictability, a water fight begins …

On the still waters of Lake Annecy, we splashed and rammed and yelped and maneuvered, and as we did so, Swiss-French people on the beautiful lake's serene shores looked on in quiet bemusement, nervously yodeling to themselves. Mending their watches. Eating chocolate. You get the picture.

Diving into the lake fully clothed, we finally swam ashore, towing our unsinkable ships behind us. Climbing out of the water with my gym shoes squelching, jeans the weight of lead, and T-shirt vacuum-packed around my shivering torso, I knew it was time to confront a recurring childhood nightmare: I was going to have to Get Changed In Public.

Of course the idea is simple: You just wrap a towel around you, drop your wet things surreptitiously, then hoist your dry pants dextrously up-and-under before whipping away the towel with an air of nonchalant finesse.

In the privacy of my own bedroom, I have achieved the above procedure towel-free and semi-comatose most mornings of my life. But the moment there are people looking, the moment there's a towel and a crowd involved, I seem to end up flashing the world more often than a lighthouse in a twister on a very dark night indeed. The problem is my toe—my big toe—which suddenly becomes enormous. So big that my underpants catch on it every time, and this invariably leaves me hopping and flailing with my towel flapping and trailing, as I yank my pants frantically upwards in futile terror. It's enough to make a man blush on all four cheeks.

2

On the shores of Lake Annecy, I was determined to avoid exposing myself, quite literally, to such ridicule from the general public once again and decided to search out the privacy of a lavatory. I fetched my dry clothes from the car (parked below ground in a multi-story parking lot) and, dripping lake water on the concrete floor, followed signs to "Les Toilettes." Surprisingly, these led me to a pair of gleaming elevator doors. I pressed the button, the doors hummed open, and I saw before me a space that was immaculately clean, burnished bright, carpeted, and empty. If you've ever "been" in a French public lavatory, you will probably understand that I wasn't exactly looking forward to my visit, and the elevator suddenly seemed (to the part of me that is eternally and irredeemably stupid) strangely inviting, secluded, and safe.

And so, as the doors kissed shut behind me, my brain watched my body in slow-motion panic as it did something entirely dumb. As the elevator began to purr north, I dropped my wet underpants and—naked as the day I was born—started fumbling frantically for my clothes. I had just caught my boxers on my big toe, and was therefore hopping around in demented panic, like Rumplestiltskin on a nudist beach, when light suddenly filled the whole elevator. And that was the moment of mortifying shame during which I realized:

It was a glass elevator.

I was prancing around in pink terror, stark naked in a transparent box suspended from the ceiling. What is more, the particular elevator shaft in which I had chosen to undress was evidently the centerpiece of a cavernous and exceedingly busy French shopping complex. Public nudity is one thing, but this was turning out to be exhibitionism on a very grand scale indeed.

Just then, a lady in a floral headscarf happened to glance up at the cubicle gliding serenely toward the ceiling, and, as our eyes met, we both froze. Suddenly she started gesticulating wildly. A commotion was stirring, and I fell to the floor horrified, caught in the very essence of every nightmare I have ever suffered since the age of about seven. Like a demented Houdini, I was attempting to wrestle my clammy frame horizontally into my clothes, writhing with grunts and groans and praying with every breath to the King of all kings that no demonized shopper had casually "felt led" to summon the elevator to the next floor.

3

The prospect of such an encounter brought me to my senses, and with my trousers wrapped backwards around my ankles, I fumbled frantically for a "down" button, pushing it relentlessly until the glass box grudgingly paused, sighed, and then began to descend grumbling and mumbling slowly back down toward the ground floor. As it did so, the elevator's solitary, semi-naked occupant clung to the carpet like Spiderman peering in terror at the chattering crowds below. Some were standing around staring and still pointing in disbelief, but others were continuing their business quite oblivious. As I sank below the floor, I wondered what possible explanation I could proffer should a policeman be waiting for the

English exhibitionist on the other side of those burnished doors. The headlines were inevitable: "Exhibitionist Evangelist in Elevator Shock."

And so the glass box slowed to a halt and seemed to pause for an eternity. In a moment, the doors would part like the curtains of some tawdry peepshow to reveal my fate. I caught my reflection in those gleaming doors, trying to look respectable, outraged, and innocent all at once. Trying not to look like the sort of man who accidentally exhibits himself on a shopping trip. In an elevator. Made of glass.

The doors hummed open to reveal a deserted underground parking lot. Sweet relief. A few feet above me on the shop floor, there was doubtless a commotion, but down here, all remained serene and sensible for a few more moments at least. Stepping hurriedly out of my booth, I ran to the car, fully clothed but inconsolably and eternally deranged with shame.

4

If only, I reflected later, I had taken time to examine that elevator at the most elementary level. If only I had engaged my brain before dropping my pants. But I hadn't stopped for a single second to wonder where that cubicle was headed, nor to notice the simple fact that it was made of glass (surely making it one of the worst places on earth in which to get undressed). I hadn't thought even two seconds into the future. When those doors purred shut behind me, I simply acted on instinct in response to a pressing need with results that were embarrassing to say the very least. I just hadn't thought ahead.

> **Vision:** *Act or faculty of seeing; thing seen vividly in the imagination; imaginative insight; statesmanlike foresight; sagacity in planning; the visual component of a television broadcast.*
> (*Oxford English Dictionary*)

As I stepped into that elevator that fateful day, I showed myself to be distinctly lacking in the quality of "statesmanlike foresight" and utterly devoid of "sagacity in planning." And of course, my lack of vision cost me dearly.

It's all too easy to live from week to week without foresight, insight, and vision, or with a distorted vision that surreptitiously undermines all that we do. I meet so many people who have never stopped to ask the most basic questions about the direction of their lives or the purpose for which they have been placed on earth. They live from day to day, buffeted by random circumstance, subconsciously delegating responsibility for their destiny to "fate," to a pastor, a parent, or the tedious conveyor belt of the cultural norms in which they happen to live.

𝕬 WORLD WITHOUT RESTRAINT

The Bible says very simply that without vision, "we perish" (Proverbs 29:18 KJV). Modern translations express it like this: "Where there is no revelation, the people cast off restraint." We live in a world that—for lack of vision—has cast off restraint and is dying by degrees:

5

- We lack the most basic levels of visionary foresight, destroying natural resources essential for the survival of future generations in a frenzy of self-indulgence.
- We lack spiritual foresight, too, living for the day at the expense of eternity.
- We also lack "imaginative insight," finding ourselves materially wealthy yet morally bankrupt.

𝕳OW DID THIS HAPPEN?

First, we lost our vision of God. Friedrich Nietzsche was a nineteenth century philosopher whose ideas had a profound influence on the ideology of the twentieth century. In his book, *The Gay Science*, Nietzsche described an age that believed it no longer needed God:

> "Do we hear the noise of the grave-diggers who are burying God?
> Do we not smell the divine putrefaction?—for even Gods putrefy!
> God is dead!
> God remains dead!
> And we have killed him!
> How shall we console ourselves,
> the most murderous of all murderers? …
> Is not the magnitude of this deed too great for us?
> Shall we not ourselves have to become gods,
> merely to seem worthy of it?"[1]

6

Believing that God is dead, men like Hitler, who drew heavily on Nietzsche's thinking, sought to elevate a "super-race" of god-like humans to rule the world unpolluted, while others downgraded humanity to the status of amoral apes. Nietzsche's contemporary, Fyodor Dostoevsky, explored these themes repeatedly in books like *The Idiot* and *Brothers Karamazov*, asserting that without God, there can be no morality.[2] And so, in losing our vision of God, we did exactly what the Bible predicted: We cast off restraint.

Meanwhile, as Nietzsche wrote his philosophy in poems and Dostoevsky expressed his faith in novels, Charles Darwin was theorizing about the evolution of species in the theater of scientific research, intimating strongly that human beings are mere animals in a cut-throat world. We believed him and began to behave like animals more and more. After all, how could man be made in the image of a God who did not exist? Thus, in losing our vision of the dignity of humanity, we cast off restraint once again.

1. *The Gay Science*, Friedrich Nietzsche (Random House, U.S.A.: 1974).
2. In *Brothers Karamazov*, Ivan asserts that "if there is no immortality, there is no virtue." Elsewhere, in *The Idiot*, Keller explains that, "having ceased to believe in God Almighty, he had lost every vestige of morality" (Chapter 27). Dostoevsky was fascinated with this idea that "without God everything is permitted" and that morality becomes meaningless. Of course, this philosophical position went on to inspire the French Existentialist movement—most notably the writings of Jean Paul Sartre.

AUGUSTINE OF HIPPO

The Bible describes an era when the people of Israel had no king, and as a result: "everyone did as he saw fit" (Judges 17:6). We live in a time of similar moral relativism because we have no king. Without the constraints of higher accountability, we wander around this new century in a state of spiritual anarchy: not free, but lost.

Fifteen hundred years before Nietzsche, Dostoevsky, and Darwin, an African born between the Mediterranean Sea and the Sahara desert wrote this:

> "People travel to wonder,
> at the height of the mountains,
> at the huge waves of the seas,
> at the long courses of the rivers,
> at the vast compass of the ocean,
> at the circular motion of the stars,
> and they pass themselves by without wondering."

The author of these words—St. Augustine—was a man whose vision of God instilled a vision for the wonder of humanity, too. In his life, we see the biblical correlation between revelation and restraint graphically outworked. As a young man, he traveled to Carthage to study, and there he found himself thrust into "a hissing cauldron of lust."[3] Augustine was intellectually brilliant, but found himself drowning "in the whirlpools of vice," fathering an illegitimate son along the way. Augustine, for all his abilities, was a man "without restraint."

When Augustine moved to Milan to become a professor, he met Ambrose, the renowned bishop of that city. He was impressed immediately by the great man's preaching and was soon provoked at a deeper level by the message of the Gospel

---

3. *The Confessions of St. Augustine*, tr. R.S. Pine-Coffin (Penguin, Baltimore, MD: 1961) lll.1, p. 55.

itself. Confronted by the stark challenges of Christian commitment, Augustine famously prayed: "Give me chastity and self control, but not yet."

Unlike so many people today, Augustine understood that becoming a Christian would mean a lifetime of submission to Christ as Lord. He carefully counted the cost of apprenticing himself to Jesus and realized that it would not—could not—be cheap. His inner battle finally reached its dramatic climax on a summer's day in the year 386. Sitting in a pleasant garden, Augustine found himself in a state of great spiritual distress so that "a huge storm rose up within me bringing with it a huge downpour of tears."[4] At that moment, as the brilliant hedonist sobbed out his inner turmoil, banging his head and even tearing at his hair, the singsong voice of a child came drifting across the garden. "Take it and read it. Take it and read it," sang the unseen child, and obediently, Augustine opened his Bible and read the very first words he saw: "not in orgies and drunkenness," he read, "not in sexual immorality and debauchery, not in dissension and jealousy. Rather, clothe yourselves with the Lord Jesus Christ."

8

"It was as though," he recalled later, "my heart was filled with a light of confidence and all the shadows were swept away."[5]

With revelation came a new restraint, as Augustine began to clothe himself with the Lord Jesus Christ (Romans 13:12). The man who had struggled for so long with his own sexuality and pride began to grow in discipline and humility. Years later, he even placed a sign on his dining room table to remind himself not to gossip:

> *"Whoever thinks that he is able*
> *to nibble at the life of absent friends*
> *must know that he is unworthy of this table."*

Augustine spurned the fine robes of high office to dress in simple clothes, and

---

4. *Confessions*, tr. E.M. Blaiklock (Thomas Nelson, Nashville, TN: 1983) VIll. Vll, p. 196.
5. Ibid, p. 181.

every year, he would celebrate the anniversary of his ordination with a banquet for the poor. It is clear that in the most intimate details of his life—dinner conversation, the clothes he chose to wear, and the celebration of anniversaries—Augustine had found in Christ a vision that inspired and empowered him, as nothing else could, to live beautifully.

Sixteen hundred years after Augustine, it is still true that when a man or a woman receives a true vision of Christ, he or she also finds a life worth living—"For I know the plans I have for you," declares the Lord, "plans to prosper you and not to harm you, plans to give you hope and a future" (Jeremiah 29:12).

Nietzsche predicted that, as a result of the "death of God," there would be an outbreak of "universal madness." In the wake of Hitler, Stalin, and Mao, as we look around at escalating obesity and suicide rates in the West versus starvation and death in less developed parts of the world, we are perhaps forced to accept that Nietzsche's prediction has come to pass.

9

Having foreseen such insanity, Nietzsche himself went mad—possibly from the syphilis he had contracted as a student. Twelve years later, with an ultimate twist of irony, he was buried in a Christian ceremony next to the graves of his father and grandfather—both of whom had been Lutheran pastors.

We live in a perishing world, a world that has indeed "cast off restraint," a world in desperate need of a God it no longer really believes in.

But while we may doubt God, He still believes in us. He still invites ordinary people to "come follow me." And when He finds such people, they may be apparent saints like Mary the mother of Jesus or sinners such as Mary Magdalene, Saul, or a sex-mad student like Augustine. But the eyes of the Lord are still searching out those willing to live their lives above the gunnels of mediocrity and beyond the realms of inevitability. In our cynical age, God is looking for those naïve enough to believe that the world can still be changed, those simple fools whose vision is to live and die for Christ alone.

ℭYNICISM

We are predisposed to cynicism because we don't have an all-consuming cause the way previous generations did. Instead we have trends. We have products and technologies. We have our immediate circle of friends. But we don't have A Cause—not one that demands our lives and calls us to sacrifice ourselves for something bigger than our own little selves. We were never called up to fight for freedom. No ration books. No Cuban Missile Crisis. No man on the moon. No Martin Luther King, Jr. Just disposable heroes sponsoring products. Stuff. Things that come and go.

And the truth is that we like it this way. So we protect ourselves from the zeal of over-commitment with a worldview that undermines absolutes of any kind. We get bored watching war in real-time on TV. We turn the Gospel of salvation into a lapel badge and a sanitized program. We're like the kids at school who maybe know the answer but don't want to put their hands up in case they look too keen.

As a result of this comfortable, cause-lite existence of ours, we are living like ghosts in time, happy to consume and be consumed without a thoughtful vision or an all-consuming passion. The glass elevator of human history may well prove embarrassing for a generation like ours, naked of ideals and unsure about its own destiny and direction.

𝔍 BONSAI, YOU TREE

I was admiring a friend's cute little bonsai tree when I noticed a storm gathering outside. As the first flurry of rain crackled against the window, I found myself gazing out at an old, gnarled oak tree standing silhouetted against the darkening sky. Sometimes I feel like the bonsai—a pruned and pampered indoor miniature, a cartoon of those great, wizened giants of another age, weathering storms, defying the lightning, standing strong because they were rooted deep. Where, we wonder, is the cause worth braving the elements of our time?

Perhaps it's time to make a simple decision: that we will believe the things we believe and therefore allow them to overwhelm us and to doubt the things we doubt and therefore deny them their power. Perhaps it's time for the shy kid to raise her hand in class and dare to be wrong, dare to incur a little ridicule for seeming too keen.

Have we the courage to radiate our passion in such a cynical age, to live for Jesus "dangerously, obsessively, and undeniably"? Not for money, not for fame, not for career, not for popularity? To live our lives for Jesus Christ alone? It seems to me that to do less is to be less than human. It is to cast off restraint. It is to perish. But to live that dream is eternal.

🕮IVING BEAUTIFULLY

In every generation, it has, without exception, been those who dared to live with an irrepressible dream who made history. A peripheral glimpse at the story of any family, city, or nation reveals the undiminished power of people with a vision to transform the environment in which they find themselves.

In 1922, a twelve-year-old girl called Agnes made a simple decision to live her life for God and the poor. From that moment on, she pursued this vision with fierce determination each day, so that at the time of her death, Agnes Gonxha left a legacy of 517 missions, orphanages, schools, and homes caring for the dying, despised, and forgotten in a hundred countries. Accepting the Nobel Peace Prize in 1979, Mother Teresa (as she was better known) urged the gathered dignitaries to "live life beautifully ..." because "God loves us, and we have an opportunity to love others as He loves us, not in big things, but in small things with great love."

🕮 VISION REALLY DOES HAVE THE POWER TO CHANGE THE WORLD.

- In the 1940s, Winston Churchill faced a "monstrous tyranny, never surpassed in the dark, lamentable catalogue of human crime." Yet, against all odds, he maintained his vision of "victory, victory at all costs, victory in spite of all terror, victory no matter how long and hard the road may be …"[6]

- In the 1950s, William John Clifton Haley, Jr. and his band The Saddlemen renamed themselves "Bill" and "The Comets" respectively and released *Rock Around The Clock*—the first great rock 'n' roll record that would sell twenty-five million copies, triggering a cultural revolution.

12

- In the 1960s, a young American pastor traveled some six million miles, preaching twenty-five hundred times and getting imprisoned twenty times before being killed in 1968. His name, of course, was Martin Luther King, Jr., and his irrepressible dream of racial equality galvanized the Civil Rights movement peacefully and powerfully around the world.

- The 1970s barely noticed prisoner 46664, a political activist permitted only one visitor a year for thirty minutes. However, the twenty-seven years he spent in jail became the crucible that refined Nelson Mandela's vision and transformed him from an angry revolutionary into a dignified statesman capable of leading South Africa into democracy.

- In the 1980s, a particle physicist called Tim Berners-Lee developed the world's first hypertext-based network "browser" software, arguably making him the inventor of the World Wide

6. Churchhill's first speech as prime minister of the United Kingdom, May 13, 1940, to the House of Commons.

Web. With a vision of the Internet's potential to connect people, he selflessly insisted that the technology be kept in the public domain so that anyone anywhere could use and improve it. And thus the information revolution began.

- In the 1990s, Anne Pettifor told a distinguished gathering that "if you want to make God laugh, you should tell Him your plans for the future." She proceeded to plan hilarious "ways to celebrate the birth of Christ by giving a billion people a debt-free start"[7] to the third millennium. Within four years, Anne, with a little help from celebrities like Bono, had achieved the unthinkable. The Jubilee Campaign had somehow persuaded the richest countries in the world to wipe out a staggering $111 billion of the debt crippling the poorest countries.

And what of this decade? Perhaps readers of this book will be noted by future generations as some of the great visionaries of our time. God has often called ordinary people to live with extraordinary vision, and it can happen again.

INSPIRATION AND REVELATION

However, you may well be looking at this list of world-changers with a growing sense of inadequacy. *That's all very well for them*, you think, *but I'm no Nelson Mandela, Bill Haley, or Mother Teresa. I'm just me!* We all believe in God's power to change the world through others; we just struggle to believe in His power to do it through us.

Of course, an era-defining achievement generally requires exceptionally gifted and focused people (such as the ones listed above) to see it through. We cannot all be like that, and it would be a sad society if we were!

---

7. Talk given to SEDOS (Service of Documentation and Studies of Mission), February 17, 1999, by Anne Pettifor, International Director of the Jubilee 2000 Campaign.

But when a vision comes to us not as human aspiration, but as divine revelation—then the whole equation changes. God's commission always comes with His provision: He promises to supply our needs, to sustain us, to renew our strength, to redeem our mistakes, to use our weaknesses, and—best of all—to journey with us. He uses the weak and the foolish to confound the wise, ordinary people to do extraordinary things for His glory. With God, there is no "just me." Our protestations of stupidity simply fall on the deaf ears of grace.

In a cynical age, we must remind ourselves constantly that idealism is not wrong, neither is it unrealistic, provided it is God's idealism and not ours.

Christians have cause—more than any others—to live with great vision and hope. Churches could be hot-houses of creative dissent, eccentricity, passionate perseverance, and fun. Here is Handel humming some new tune to himself, Michelangelo scribbling on envelopes, Teresa of Avila lost in wonder, Augustine in the pulpit. William Booth is here with the bread, and Bono is swigging the wine. An African child rides Desmond Tutu's laughing shoulders; Billy Graham stands with his well-thumbed Bible, Martin Luther King, Jr. with his dream, Mother Teresa by the door.

14

Here you are and here I am in the congregation, no more ordinary than those above, dreaming and scheming and relentlessly asking "Why?" "like little children" (Matthew 18:3). Christians may take life with all its terror and all its joy as a great and dark adventure, hand-in-hand with the One for whom "nothing is impossible" (Luke 1:37) and through whom "all things work together for good" (Romans 8:28). Christians in such company really can dare to be different, to doubt and to wonder and to rattle the cages of social constraint.

15

"We are the music-makers,
And we are the dreamers of dreams,
Wandering by lone sea-breakers,
And sitting by desolate streams.
World-losers and world-forsakers,
Upon whom the pale moon gleams;
Yet we are the movers and shakers,
Of the world forever, it seems."
(Arthur O'Shaughnessy)

CHAPTER TWO
THE VISION IS JESUS

A distinguished art critic was studying an exquisite painting by the Italian Renaissance master Filippino Lippi one day. He stood in London's National Gallery gazing at the fifteenth century depiction of Mary holding the infant Jesus on her lap, with saints Dominic and Jerome kneeling nearby, but the painting troubled him. There could be no doubting Lippi's skill, his use of color or composition. But the proportions of the picture were slightly wrong: The hills in the background seemed exaggerated, as if they might topple out of the frame at any minute onto the gallery's polished floor. And the two kneeling saints just looked awkward and uncomfortable.

Robert Cumming was not the first to criticize Lippi's work for its poor perspective, but he may well be the last to do so, because at that moment he had a revelation. It suddenly occurred to him that the problem might be his. The painting he was analyzing with clinical objectivity was not just another piece of religious art hanging in a gallery alongside other comparative works. It had never been intended to come anywhere near a gallery. Lippi's painting had been commissioned as an altarpiece, intended to hang in a place of prayer.

And so, self-consciously, the dignified art critic in the public gallery dropped to his knees before the painting. And suddenly he saw what generations of art critics had missed. From his newfound position of humility, Robert Cumming found himself gazing up at a perfectly proportioned piece. The foreground had moved naturally to the background, while the saints seemed settled—their awkwardness, like the painting itself, having turned to grace. And as for Mary, she now looked intently and kindly directly at him as he knelt at her feet between saints Jerome and Dominic.

It was not the perspective of the painting that had been wrong all these years— it was the perspective of the people looking at it. Robert Cumming on bended knee had found a beauty that Robert Cumming the proud art critic could not. All these years, the joke had been upon the succession of experts standing, studying, and analyzing instead of kneeling humbly in prayer.

SEEING AS WE ARE

The French existential novelist Anais Nin wrote in her diary, "We don't see things as they are, we see them as we are."[1] When—like that art critic—we drop the façade of pompous posturing and fall to the floor in prayer, we gain a new perspective on life that brings out the beauty and grace in a world that had previously seemed so chaotic. Outwardly, nothing has changed: We close our Bibles, leave the worship time, return from retreat, and the same old struggles and distortions present themselves as truth.

18

But while they may not have changed, we have.

Now we gaze up at the picture and find beauty and perspective where once we could see only faults and flaws. What's more, we begin to understand that we have a place in the overall composition of the picture—kneeling among the saints in worship. And as we do so, the most wonderful shift takes place: Our vision is renewed to see Jesus right in the center of it all.

REVELATION AND IMAGINATION

Our perspective will be shaped, consciously or subconsciously, positively or negatively, by the initial position we adopt before God, His Word, and His

---

1. Introduction to *The Diary of Anais Nin*, 1931-1934, Ed. Gunther Stuhlmann (Swallow Press: 1966).

world. A commercial for Caterpillar clothing declares, "We shape the things we build, thereafter they shape us." It's vital to get our starting points right in prayer and humility, lest, like countless others, we live our lives and give our all for a misguided cause or a distorted vision.

When a vision is born in the pride of a prayer-less imagination, it is nothing more than a projection of the self—what Freud called the ego. Self-projected vision is beamed indiscriminately onto the world by an inner drive to be larger than life in every conversation, in every context, and in posterity, too. Self-projected vision is an empire-building compulsion; it comes not to serve, but to be served. The great tragedy of such self-referenced visionaries is the loneliness that awaits them at the end of the road as a diminutive Wizard of Oz finally steps out from behind the apparatus of his dreams.

Sadly, the Church is full of people whose motives are fundamentally egotistical, while their vocabulary is entirely Christian and their ministries apparently fruitful. "I can see it now," said Jesus, "at the Final Judgment thousands strutting up to me and saying, 'Master, we preached the Message, we bashed the demons, our God-sponsored projects had everyone talking.' And do you know what I am going to say? 'You missed the boat. All you did was use me to make yourselves important. You don't impress me one bit. You're out of here'" (Matthew 7:22-23 MSG).

Many will realize too late that it is not enough to have a vision, not even a vision that is expressly Christian. All my achievements will mean nothing on that day when Jesus looks me in the eye with a single question: Did we know each other?

Our vision as Christians is not of a program, a path, or a plan for global domination; it is of a Person. And He looks at us now as we look at Him and says very simply, "Come follow me." We know not where, only that it will be with Him.

THE ENCOUNTER

And now we must come to perhaps the most painful part of this book, even more challenging than the later chapters on discipleship and covenant. Here we must stop hiding behind analogies about fifteenth century paintings, and twentieth century glass elevators, and face up to the fundamental question of the human soul, a question that many people—even Christian leaders—spend their entire lives running from. And it is a question that comes to us directly from the lips of Christ.

But before I bring you the question, I invite you to pause for a few moments, to hush the internal rush, and to prepare yourself for total honesty.

Please stop being a Christian for these moments. Drop that and every title you carry: mother, leader, student, boss—whatever. Come right now as you truly are. And as you remove these covers, allow sin to float to the surface. A callous comment. A lustful thought. A selfish act. A secret grudge. Small attitudes and actions you manage to excuse most of the time to everyone but yourself in the middle of the night. Don't delve for sin, but admit what's there. Honest. No masks.

Take a minute before you read any more to be still. What's troubling you? Name the bruises of recent rejection, the selfish impulses, the butterflies of hope. Come as you are. No more or less.

This is important, because the exercise we are about to do could just be another chapter in a book, or it could change your life, revolutionize your vision, and prepare you for the greatest encounter of them all.

If you're anything like me, you may by now be thinking, *Okay, I'll read it quickly now and do the prayer bit later.* But please don't defer this. Let's do this in "real time." Nothing is more important than this encounter, so resign yourself if necessary to being a little late for the next appointment in your day. If the world can wait for a Super Bowl game, or a traffic jam, or a pregnant woman, it can wait for you now. The truth is, you see, that many people defer this encounter their whole lives.

To prepare yourself for the question that is coming from Christ, there is one you must first ask yourself and seek to answer with utter truthfulness:

>*Do I really hunger for Jesus Christ?*
>
>Think about it.
>
>*Am I really hungry for more of Jesus in my life?*

And if you answered an immediate yes, without any hesitation, let me just say this as gently as I can: Unless you are a new believer, you have probably by now built quite a coherent identity around yourself defined by this word "Christian." And it's easy to end up a bit like one of professor Pavlov's (highly trained) dogs, which would salivate at the mere ring of a bell, whether or not there was food on the table. Sometimes we can answer automatically and unthinkingly to questions that carry lots of religious trigger words—and I've just given you a classic example of the genre! So let me rephrase the question like this:

>What made you happy this week?

Was it an hour you had alone with Jesus in prayer? Was it a chance you took to serve Him secretly in some small way, offering it up as a childish gift for Him alone? Or did your joy this week primarily spring from a new CD, a shopping trip, accessing the next level on a video game, or a pizza in front of the *Frasier* re-run?

The answers to questions like these enable us to gauge our spiritual hunger:

- Am I craving, and so creating, time alone with Jesus in prayer?
- Is He more important to me than my partner, my family, and my friends?
- Do I find Christ's name on my lips throughout the day, or only in overtly sacred contexts?
- Is He my last thought at night and my first in the morning as I stumble to the bathroom?
- Do I make time to pore over His biography?
- Is my prayer life garrisoned into occasional blocks of time, or

do I also find myself conversing with Him about ridiculous trivia throughout the day?

No one will answer an unequivocal "yes" to all the right questions all the time, so please don't beat yourself up if you're now realizing that there is a reality gap in your desire for Christ.

The aim of this exercise is not to discourage you, but rather to encourage you to come to Christ now in honesty, with all your defenses down, perhaps admitting to Him that you don't actually want Him as much as you say you do, and certainly that you are not as righteous as the image you project to others. Instead, you come to Him like the tax collector without pretension in weakness and need:

Just as I am, without one plea,
But that Thy blood was shed for me,
And that Thou bidst me come to Thee,
O Lamb of God, I come, I come.

THE QUESTION

Next I invite you to imagine that you are looking beyond the words on this page, into the face of Jesus, and as you do so, His eyes are kindly, quietly burning into yours. You can feel them like lasers probing your heart. And as He looks at you, hear Him speaking your name. Notice how softly He repeats it. But as He says your name, you glimpse a slight furrowing of the brow and a hint of pain dulling the kindness in His eyes. Seeing this, you become slightly self-conscious, aware that you are naked of ambition and pretense, nobody but yourself alone with Him. And Jesus is looking more deeply into you now than anyone has ever done before. He speaks your name with that hint of pain, and then comes the question we have been preparing ourselves to hear—the challenge more painful than any other.

The question is this:

"Do you love me?"

That's it. Just four words. Big deal.

And of course you know the answer right away. With a relieved smile, you reply immediately: "Yes, Lord, You know I do." You've sung it a million times in church, and so, without a second thought, you say, "Yes." We all say, "Yes." Hey—we're people who read Christian books! "Yes, Lord, of course I love You!"

But the Lord's gaze is unbroken, and He is not mirroring your grin. He seems troubled by your reply. The question is coming again.

"Do you *really* love me?"

A second time—does He doubt me? A little offended, you pause before answering, and as you do so, the question begins to penetrate. The intensity in Jesus' eyes is even greater, the dark probing lasers of His question going deeper still. And of course, you know why He doubts your first reply. He of all people sees those sins you've allowed to float to the surface. This is the question God has been wanting to ask for a while now, and at last you are coming to Him with ears to hear and a vulnerable heart that will not simply dodge the question without a little thought. It's a real question from a Friend you sometimes hurt and a Lord who knows you deny Him more often than you let on. Hence the pain when He speaks your name. As you reflect on these things—your quick confessions of love, your easy infidelity, and your embarrassment now—you notice Him nodding very slightly as if reading your mind. And maybe, just maybe, there is the faintest mist of a tear appearing in His eyes.

Whisper your reply.

Perhaps there is a hint of pain and shame in your features now, because something changes in the face before you. You see tears welling up, unmistakeably, but instead of sadness, there is joy. The eyes of your Lord looking at you seem now to have melted into such kind puddles of utter affection that you feel loved as deeply as you realize you are known. Of course, you understand by now that the question must come a third time, but you never expected there to be such surprising vulnerability in the One who asks:

"Do you even *like* me?"

Suddenly, with that vulnerable, all knowing question, an avalanche of emotion surges in through your eyes and pounds into the caverns of your soul. Something—call it love, pain, joy, relief—just wells up inside you as if a great wave has hit the rocks and now spumes up into the sky through some secret funnel.

And this time your answer to the question comes from the depth of your being—a place deeper than your public pretending, and somehow even deeper than the sins that lie beneath as well. Your answer erupts from the inner sanctum of your soul, the core of your being, like an explosion of champagne, unashamed and unreserved:

"Yes, Lord, yes! I love You. I love You because You know all things, and You still love me. I am loved. I am known. And what can I do but love You back?"[2]

And one day soon, not so long from now, this same Jesus will look at you with those eyes "like blazing fire," and He will say: "Yes, my friend, I knew you. Come, today you will be with me in paradise. Come to the place I have prepared for you here in heaven (John 14:2). Come follow me, you who are blessed by my Father" (Matthew 25:34).

And on that day, you will follow. Not for the first time.

---

2. This exercise reflects the interchange between Peter and Jesus (John 21:15-17) after Peter's denial.

CLARITY OF VISION

Brennan Manning tells the story of John Kavanaugh, a brilliant ethicist who went to live for three months in Mother Teresa's "House of the Dying" in Calcutta on a personal pilgrimage to find vital guidance—a clear vision for the rest of his life. On his very first morning, Mother Teresa asked Kavanaugh, as she asked everyone, "What can I do for you?" He requested prayer, but she wanted to know what kind.

Without hesitation, Kavanaugh, who had traveled thousands of miles on his quest, replied, "Please pray that I get clarity for the future."

"No!" retorted Mother Teresa emphatically, "I will not do that ... Clarity is the last thing you are clinging to and must let go of."

"But you always seem to have clarity," Kavanaugh pleaded, a little taken aback. With a twinkle in her eye, Mother Teresa laughed, "I have *never* had clarity; what I have always had is trust. So I will pray you trust God."[3]

When Jesus calls us to follow Him, we want clarity: to assess our options, set expectations, and know our boundaries. But God's route from A to C is rarely via B. His voice is rarely unmistakeable. His Word often raises more questions than answers. We ask for guidance expecting a roadmap, or at least a sign, and He gives us His hand and the dimmest of torches.

My three-year-old son Danny is categorically one of the cutest human beings on planet earth right now. He has big hazel-brown eyes and hair that is so fair it's almost white and often impossible to tame with a hairbrush. Most of the time it just stands on end like Einstein's. Like most kids his age, he loves going to the park to play on the slides and swings; in fact, it is probably his favorite pastime in the world. And he knows that if he wants to go, all he has to do is stretch his arms up toward me and say (very plaintively), "Daddeeee? Daniel want to go to park." He doesn't know the way to the park, but he does know that in my arms, he somehow gets there. Instead of directions, he has Daddy, and that is enough.

---

3. Brennan Manning, *Ruthless Trust* (SPCK, London: 1992) p. 5.

It was doubting Thomas, who said to Jesus, "Lord, we don't know where you are going, so how can we know the way?" and Jesus answered, "I am the way ... anyone who has seen me has seen the Father" (John 14). When we turn our faces to Christ, He carries us, because He is "the way." He takes us to places we could not find on our own. And even if we could, wouldn't we rather be carried in His arms?

The heartbeat of our faith is not achieving great things *for* God, nor is it doing great things *with* God. Our deepest longing is simply to be with God, to know Him as Friend and Father, to trust Him as Savior, and thus, to obey Him as Lord.

"The Vision" is not the vision. My faith is not staked on the fulfillment of my call. The vision is Jesus. He is the fixed point in a swirling sea of worthy dreams. He calls me to follow, to focus on Him, to bow the knee before the altar-piece, to orbit His burning star. When we "fix our eyes upon Jesus, the author and perfecter of our faith," there will be many consequences, many aspirations—there may even be a great deal of activity and achievement. But these are just fractals of grace, and while others may applaud our apparent success, our plumb line is His presence, and our focus is His face.

26

How wonderful to be welcomed at the end of life's journey with cries of recognition: "I knew you! Well done, my good and faithful child." Hearing this exclamation, you will probably wonder for just a moment if God has gotten His facts right. You may even feel compelled to protest your guilt—the embarrassing litany of sin and stupidity that you have brought to His attention a thousand times before (admittedly in less auspicious surroundings). But He will simply scoop you up in His arms as you splutter your surprise, and—in front of all those big people with such big ministries—the Father will carry you—little you—to a joyful place you could never, ever have found on your own. Not in a month of Sundays. Not in a lifetime of achievement. Only in His arms.

"And they shall live with his face in view, and that they belong to him will show on their faces" (Revelation 22:4-5).[4]

---

4. A translation from the Greek of Revelation 22:4-5 by Dallas Willard in *The Divine Conspiracy* (HarperCollins Publishers, New York, NY: 1998) p. 409.

CHAPTER THREE
I AM THE VISION

In J.R.R. Tolkien's classic tale *The Hobbit*, Bilbo Baggins lives agreeably in his burrow at Bag End, Hobbiton Hill, until one fateful spring morning, his idyll is shattered by the arrival of Gandalf. "There is more to you than you know," declares the kind old wizard, remembering Bilbo's parentage. From his father, Bilbo had undoubtedly inherited the easy-going nature of most hobbits, but on his mother's side, he hailed from the intrepid Took clan, ancient defenders of the Shire. And standing there that morning, Gandalf senses that there is a Tookish thirst for adventure beating secretly in the heart of gentle Bilbo Baggins.[1]

I believe that God often looks at us the way Gandalf looked at Bilbo, and He says, "There is more to you than you know." He sees in your heart the understandable yearning for comfort and conformity: the plans, the savings, the predictable wish list of a tidy life. But He also sees in your soul the thirst for adventure. This internal tension reflects the different blood in our veins—our dual heritage. In Adam, there is the primal drive to survive, to protect, to nurture, and to hide. But we also have the healing, cleansing, life-giving blood of Christ in our veins, pulsing with the desire to glorify God in a life fully lived. The respectable Pharisee, Nicodemus, on his own spiritual quest, came to find Jesus one night, wrapped in the cover of darkness, and he was confronted with the ultimate indignity: "You must be born again," Jesus tells him unapologetically, adding, "The wind blows wherever it pleases. You hear its sound, but you cannot tell where it

---

1. This parable is explored beautifully in Ken Gire's *Windows of the Soul* (Zondervan, Michigan: 1996) p.48.

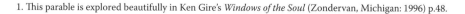

comes from or where it is going. So it is with everyone born of the Spirit."

According to Jesus, those born of the Holy Spirit will be spontaneous, unpredictable, and wild like the wind. Joel prophesied that the outpouring of the Spirit in the last days would interrupt people in every walk of life with fresh vision and surprising dreams. In the light of such biblical depictions of the Spirit-filled life, it's disappointing—to say the least—that so many of the churches and individuals currently defining themselves as Charismatic or Pentecostal are so mind-numbingly predictable and unimaginative. Where are those in our day born of the Spirit who will blow wherever He pleases and go whenever He moves?

CALL OF THE WILD

I am told that when the winter winds rise and wild geese migrate overhead, the cockerels and even the fat and stupid chickens in the barns below sometimes see the sight and fling themselves into the air flapping frantically south. We all sense this call of the wild, the lure to rise on the thermals of God, but only those born of the Spirit can stretch their wings and fly.

Whenever the Spirit truly fills a person, something Tookish awakes. God's original vision for their lives is activated, and they begin to dream, to adventure, to live in the exciting spontaneity of God's leading.

When Bilbo opened his door to Gandalf, the adventure began, and it started, as such things always do, with disruption. As the wizard stepped through the hobbit's circular door, twelve dwarfs scurried in with him and proceeded to make themselves very much at home. Bilbo set about trying to be hospitable (as hobbits do), but eventually ran out of food and energy, too. Eventually, he sat himself down exhausted, and the dwarfs began to sing. As Bilbo sat listening to those ancient songs, "something Tookish woke up inside him, and he wished to go and see the great mountains, and hear the pine trees and the waterfalls, and explore the caves, and wear a sword instead of a walking stick."

Once upon a time, God's vision was to give you life, and—mystery of mysteries—a tiny heart began to beat in your mother's womb. But His purpose was, and is, to give you even more than life. His vision—in fact, His glory—is to give you life to the full! He serenades you with the call of the wild, and whenever you hear the sound, as deep calls to deep, it causes Tookish blood to coarse through your veins, stirring you spiritually and creatively, invoking the risk-taking part of you, the part that was born to wear a sword and not a walking stick, the part that longs to rise and fly with the wild geese to summer climes, the part that can be unpredictable as the wind.

Most of the time, however, we are predictably burrowed away in our hobbit holes, content and safe for a while at least. But then along comes the stranger who knows us better than we know ourselves. He looks in our eyes and says that there is more to us than we know. There is nothing wrong with the walking stick. Nothing wrong with the shire. In fact, these things are good. It's simply that they are not enough; they are a half-life, a safe life, an earthly life, but they fall short of the overflowing life that glorifies God.

Brennan Manning, the author who is now in his seventies and has lived one of the fullest lives imaginable, reflects that "the defining moments of my life have not been my sins or my successes. They've been a depressingly small number of decisions that involved real risk." Christ is not a passive Savior sitting still in some cosmic comfy chair. Our God is dynamic; He is a creative force, the ultimate visionary, always on the move, and if we want to know Him and be with Him, we will have to follow Him wherever He is going next. This is the adventure of discipleship.

𝕁𝕝 FULL LIFE

In the '90s cult classic TV series *Buffy the Vampire Slayer*, the blood-slurping Londoner Spike makes a surprising admission:

"We like to talk big. Vampires do:
'I'm going to destroy the world.'
That's just tough-guy talk,
strutting around with your friends over a pint of blood.
The truth is: I like this world. You've got ...
dog racing, Manchester United. And you've got people.
Billions of people walking around like Happy Meals with legs.
It's alright here.
But then someone comes along with a vision ..."

Billions of us really do walk around like "Happy Meals with legs," being consumed by a consumer society, until "someone comes along with a vision ..." Whenever a person wakes up to discover that things don't have to be the way they currently are and that they have a part to play in changing things for good, Satan's annoyance is almost as great as God's joy, because we begin to live the life for which we were designed.

St. Irenaeus of Lyons lived just one hundred and fifty years after Jesus, in Gaul (modern day France), and "may justly be called the first biblical theologian," having been the first to quote the New Testament unequivocally as scripture.[2] In tone, his teaching was earthier than that of his fellow Church Fathers, Origen and Tertullian, and theologically more relational, less transactional, than that of Augustine. I tell you all this because I want you to know that this is a man you can trust. And I want you to trust him, because what I am about to convey to you is a revelation that really could revolutionize your understanding of how God sees you. In his treatise, "Against The Heresies," Irenaeus made an observation that, almost two thousand years later, remains simply breathtaking in its implications for our lives. He wrote: "The glory of God is man fully alive, and the life of man is the vision of God."[3]

2. *The Early Christian Fathers*, Ed. Henry Bettenson (Oxford University Press: 1956) p. 13.
3. "Adversus Haereses," IV.xx.6 cited Ibid. p. 76. This is the popularized version of the more exact translation: "For the glory of God is a living man; and the life of man is the vision of God."

Stop and think about it for a moment. In fact, start thinking about it for a lifetime ... While my vision—the Christian vision—is Christ, His vision is ... me! His vision is not just some cosmic master plan for benevolent domination, nor is it filled with those legions of angels about His throne. God's vision is filled with His children, and His greatest delight—His highest joy—is to see us fully alive.

When the prophet Isaiah "saw the Lord seated on a throne, high and exalted" (6:1), he made an extraordinary discovery about heaven's priorities. In that moment, Isaiah—like Irenaeus—discovered that God's vision is not consumed with Himself, but rather with His creation: "Whom shall I send?" cries the Lord, His eyes scanning the earth, "who will go for us?" God's heart is not locked away in the glory of His home, where smoke fills the temple and unceasing worship shakes the doorposts. God's heart beats in heaven for the people He has made. Even the Seraphs around God's throne envision "the whole earth ... full of his glory" (6:3).

Some gods are glorified by a golden idol in a temple, or by a teenager strapping explosives to her trembling physique, or by the paparazzi around them like flies. But not our God. He is the Lord of such lords, and He is glorified not by death and dotage, but by vibrant lives overflowing with His presence.

This is the express reason Jesus came to earth: "that they may have life, and have it to the full" (John 10:10). As we prioritize Jesus, we come alive, because God's original and ultimate purpose in making us is unlocked. Conversely, when we fix our vision on anyone or anything other than Christ, we break the cycle of grace, spiraling out of God's will and falling short of His best for us. So many people, even high achievers, live sad lives "of quiet desperation" simply because they are pursuing a vision in life that is not the one for which they were created.[4] "Look at that man, bloated by self-importance but soul-empty," laughs the prophet Habakkuk, "but the person in right standing before God through loyal and steady believing is fully alive, really alive" (2:4 MSG).

4. Henry David Thoreau, *Walden* (Dover Publications: 1995).

Habakkuk talks about being "really alive." Irenaeus refers to the glory of "man fully alive." Jesus says He came to bring "life to the full." What does this tantalizing phrase actually mean? What kind of life is it that God considers "full"?

In the rest of this chapter, I am going to explore just three of the keys to discovering the kind of amazing life that glorifies God and fulfills Christ's mission in coming to earth:

- A full life is secure.
- A full life is celebratory.
- A full life is sacrificial.

1. A FULL LIFE IS SECURE.

Whenever my son Daniel hurls himself like a demented lemming from the top bunk into my arms, he screams and laughs with uninhibited delight. He is experiencing one of life's moments of exhilaration, as does a bungee jumper or a bride at the altar. But should he be silly enough to hurl himself down without me there, should the bride not find her groom, or the bungee cord turn out to be broken, the same scenario becomes entirely different.

Being fully alive begins with a sense of security. We derive this from many sources, especially the love of friends and family, but we only find total security in those "everlasting arms" ready to catch us whenever we jump from the top bunk and ready to comfort us should we happen to fall. The discovery that nothing can separate us from such love seeps into our souls, gradually liberating us to live faithfully, joyfully, hopefully, and life-fully! If we don't believe in the existence of such love (or we believe with hearts too hard or too hurt to receive it), we will lack life's intended foundation stone. Something will always be missing. In our insecurity, we may then assault life in a frenzied pursuit of pleasure, but like a hungry man eating with a thick cold at the table of the greatest chef, we will be unable to discern the subtlest flavors. We will savor the feast only partially. We will live, but not fully.

But when our insecurities begin to dissipate in the arms of love (and it's never a quick process), we may well find that we are less driven and so able to enjoy a simpler, slower life. The ravenous man will continue to feast and slurp (his nose streaming and his eyes watering) at the table of the top chef, while we eat far simpler food, but with greater delight.

A.W. Tozer famously said that the most important thing about you is the first thing that comes into your head when you think about God. He was right. It is only as we understand the reality of God's unshakeable love for us that discipline can flourish without becoming legalism and that we can serve Him sacrificially without striving for approval.

This book, with its call to discipleship, is therefore potentially dangerous unless you come to terms with God's approval, acceptance, and kindness, come what may. "The Vision" has excited many people in many cultures with its stirring call to arms. But before the arms of battle must come the arms of the Father's love. We are sons and daughters first and soldiers second.

The birth of Hudson, our first-born, comprehensively trashed our lives. Nothing could possibly have prepared Samie and me for the arrival of this delightful little bundle of outrageous demands in our one-bedroom, basement flat in a neighborhood of Portsmouth that is stylishly run-down, with junk shops, curry houses, and thousands of students. For Samie, pregnancy had not been easy, but after the initial trajectory of birth, we assumed that our new baby would soon settle into a serene orbit around the demands of our diaries. How deluded two people can be!

Huddy systematically woke me every two hours most nights for many months, he stopped me from leaving the house whenever I wanted to, and then, having trapped me in my own home, he would often scream very loudly in my face. It does strange things to you. For instance, I got so used to rocking his stroller backwards and forwards, backwards and forwards, that I would find myself absent-mindedly doing the same little maneuver at the supermarket with empty shopping carts. But of course, there were happier experiences, too—like the time I held him aloft until he giggled back at my grinning face. Grinning, that is, until a warm string of baby-saliva dribbled down into my open mouth. Hudson was often sick down the back of my shoulder, and in my zombie-like state, having lost all dignity, I would leave the house without bothering to change my shirt.

One hot summer's day, after changing Huddy's diaper, I decided to let him stay naked for a few minutes. I'd often seen those black-and-white posters of a hunky guy clutching a perfect little baby to his rippling six-pack stomach, and secretly, just for one brief moment of my life, I wanted to be that man. With shoulders back and belly tensed, I carried Hudson out into the garden and sauntered around casually looking masterful. It was at this point that Huddy decided to surrender control of his bowels.

I'm a lucky guy—I have many good friends. But I have a confession: If any one of them locked me in my house when I wanted to go out; if they screamed in my face at the top of their voices; if they woke me every night for months on end; if they spat in my mouth, puked on my clothes, and—um—humiliated me in public, I would really struggle to *like* them, let alone love them.

And so here we have the mystery: Hudson did all these terrible things to me repeatedly, and yet I found that I liked him. In fact, I found that I loved him. I loved him like I had never loved another human being in all my life. I loved him obsessively from an aching place inside that I had never before discovered. How could this be?

The difference, of course, is fatherhood. There is no passion in the human soul like the love that can stir the heart of a father or mother. And so I found myself lifting a simple question to God: "Surely," I said, "Surely when You say that You are my Father in heaven, You don't mean this kind of fatherhood? Surely, it's just a concept, a profound theological truth of paternity and inheritance? Surely," I hardly dared hope, "surely You do not experience this all-consuming, jealous, joyful passion in Your heart toward me that I find beating so relentlessly in my whole being for my little son?"

And of course, before the question even passed my lips, I could hear God's whisper: "Yes! That's exactly how I feel about you. That's exactly what my Fatherhood means. In fact, your experiences of fatherly love are just flickering reflections of my heart for you.

"You can hassle me continually with your prayers, clamoring for attention night and day, and I will always be there for you because I love you. You can scream in my face in fear and frustration and I will rock you in my arms until you rest. You may even soil me with the filth of your sin and I will still cherish you, I will still see your perfection and declare relentlessly to the angels around that you, my child, are mine. I have loved you with an everlasting love, I have drawn you with loving-kindness ... I will take great delight in you, I will quiet you with my love, I will rejoice over you with singing ... You are mine" (Jeremiah 31:3; Zephaniah 3:17; Isaiah 43:1).

The Apostle Paul puts it like this: "God's Spirit touches our spirits and confirms who we really are. We know who he is, and we know who we are: Father and children" (Romans 8:16 MSG). Something deep within us now begins to whisper "Abba," and we find that we long to worship, long to please Him, long to grow in His likeness and in His love.

No wonder the role of fatherhood has become such a war zone—the enemy of our souls is determined to pervert paternity and thereby deprive us of the key to our relationship with God in Christ. The word "father" has come to mean "abuse" for many. For other people, fathers are distant figures. Fathers are absent. Fathers are emotionally locked up. Fathers are busy and rarely around. Fathers discipline, while mothers nurture. Fathers are unfaithful. The list goes on describing the absolute antithesis of our Father in heaven. The predominant experience of fatherhood for many has little to do with God's love and faithfulness fleshed out in family. Instead it is a portrait of another father—the one Jesus called the "father of lies." He abuses, while God heals. He is cold-hearted, distant, and unfaithful, while God alone is love. While Satan rushes about maniacally, limited in his powers, the omnipresent God whose name is "I Am" always has time for His children.

Raniero Cantalamessa, who is preacher to the papal household, puts it beautifully: "If the written word of the Bible could be changed into a spoken word and become one single voice, this voice, more powerful than the roaring of the sea would cry out: 'The Father loves you'! (John 16:27).[5]

Jesus came to bring "life to the full" by opening the way for us to become sons and daughters of His Father, too. Jesus knew that the foundation to His own life—the foundation to any life fully lived—was and will forever be the pre-eminent discovery of the Father's love.

2. A FULL LIFE IS CELEBRATORY

Freda was a lady so full of life that her enthusiasm and sense of celebration were contagious. In the latter years of her life, she was afflicted by rheumatoid arthritis, which caused her constant pain and required her to walk with two walking sticks and to wear a neck-brace at all times. But her face would simply gleam with pleasure when anyone—especially a young person—came to talk with her. At church she would accost members of the youth group: "You're so lucky," she would beam, "to have found Jesus so young. I lived most of my life without Him, you know!"

5. Raniero Cantalamessa, *Life in Christ: A Spiritual Commentary on the Letter to the Romans* (Liturgical Press, Minnesota: 1990) p. 7.

But you would never have guessed it, for Freda was without a doubt more alive than most of the able-bodied, mega-gifted people I have ever known. And from looking at Freda alone it is clear to me that fullness of life has little to do with physical well-being and everything to do with our spiritual state.

The world loves this idea of life to the full. Not so long ago, a slogan for Pepsi claimed to have come that we might have "life to the max." Films such as *Dead Poets Society* and *American Beauty* urge us to seize the day and make the most of every opportunity. This is a great sentiment—far better than the nihilistic cry of Renton in the film *Trainspotting*: "Choose life! But why would I want to do a thing like that?" Underlying all three of these movies, and many others, is the philosophical worldview of existentialism championed in the wake of World War II by men like Jean Paul Sartre and Soren Kierkegaard.

Sartre argued that life is meaningless, absurd, a sick joke, and that it is therefore up to each one of us to stamp our own meaning upon reality. Be dramatically good: Drive your granny over to the supermarket. Be dramatically bad: Drive over your granny on the way home. It doesn't really matter. Carpe diem—seize the day.

The trouble with this approach to life, of course, is that it is all based on the false premise that there is no ultimate meaning, no purpose, no morality, no objective truth, no spiritual realm. It's a recipe for "life to the full" without the chef, or even some of the essential ingredients.

Christ weeps to see the crowds like sheep without a shepherd, multitudes lost and looking for life in all the wrong places. It's a timeless tragedy graphically depicted by the annual "pilgrimage" to the Mediterranean island of Ibiza, where the biggest nightclubs in the world create a habitat for every kind of sexual depravity and drug-fueled excess.

The crowds converge on Ibiza with an uncomplicated vision of "living it up" for a few days before returning home to more humdrum lives, sunburned and happy. They come determined to give whatever it takes to get a week or two of life to the full. And Ibiza has a lot to offer. Aside from the island's natural beauty, there is sublime music, amazing creativity, plenty of fun, and exciting fashion. How sad then that so many people, whose lives are the vision of God and who are so intent on celebration in a place with so much goodness, invariably end up empty, too drugged, drunk, or both to know their own name, let alone whether they were raped the night before. Many return home having satiated every bodily appetite, yet feeling cheap, empty, and lost.

Fullness of life has little to do with pampering the flesh and stimulating the senses, and everything to do with the forgiveness of sins and the loving purposes of the Father. We are spiritual beings—not so much creatures that have a spirit as spirits that have a body. The measure of a person's fulfillment is spiritual rather than physical, which is precisely why Freda, an elderly lady with rheumatoid arthritis, could celebrate life and radiate a joy of which Ibiza's beautiful boys and girls only dream.

And they do dream of it. Most evenings, many hundreds gather on the beach at Café Del Mar to watch the sun slowly dip behind the horizon. And generally there is a moment of unexpected stillness when the entire crowd falls silent, as though an invisible conductor has raised his hand. And sometimes as the last burning cusp of light disappears into the sea, the audience feels some primal urge to express their appreciation with a spontaneous surge of applause. Thanking the sun. Thanking the Son whose name they do not know.

If we glorify God by being fully alive, then worship becomes the natural consequence of everything we do in every aspect of life—not just the "spiritual bits." While we continue to glorify God in conventional ways, such as the singing of songs on a Sunday, we also live out His love with diligent gratitude in our workplace, in the conversations we create, the interests we pursue, the meals we eat, and the way we engage with the poor. The whole of life becomes an opportunity to rejoice, pray, and give thanks.

"Be joyful always;
pray continually;
give thanks in all circumstances;
for this is God's will for you in Christ Jesus."
(1 Thessalonians 5:16-18)

Yesterday evening was glimmering and golden, with long shadows and that brightness of light that comes only with the slight chill of early spring and the intense shimmering newness of the rising year. Unable to stay indoors, I took my boys to the harbor to watch the boats dancing on their moorings, and as we searched the shore for treasure, breathing the rusty-tang of salty air, it occurred to me that perhaps I was making my Father smile simply by seeking to celebrate the moment He had so lavishly made.

It's exhilarating to imagine the possibilities: the thought that when I light a fire on a winter's evening and the smell of wood smoke fills the house, in this simple celebratory act of life, I somehow glorify God. The thought that, when I slowly eat a bar of my favorite chocolate marzipan (as I very rarely do), or when I lose myself for a day in the wilds of the Scottish mountains, I glorify God by being for those moments fully alive. It's wonderful to think that, when I get in line at the record store clutching some new CD so tightly that I leave little circles of heat on the pristine jewel case, in these very moments of anticipation, I delight God's heart the way my own kids delight me as they excitedly await an imminent surprise. It's amazing to think that, when I lose myself in worship or find myself in the Bible, or laugh with friends until the tears run down my cheeks, I glorify the God who in the beginning made life good.

3. A FULL LIFE IS SACRIFICIAL.

Of course, there are other tears in life—seasons when there seems to be nothing at all worth celebrating, and worship is only possible as a defiant "nevertheless" to circumstance—no longer as an easy "therefore." At such times, it is tempting to stop celebrating the gift of life and to disregard Paul's admonition to "rejoice always" as unrealistic. But the writer of the letter to the Hebrews exhorts us to respond differently: "Through Jesus, therefore, let us continually offer to God a sacrifice of praise—the fruit of lips that confess his name" (Hebrews 13:15).

Notice three phrases in that verse:

- "A sacrifice of praise"—When life falls apart, it truly does become a sacrifice to praise God and to continue celebrating His gift of life in spite of the pain.
- "Through Jesus"—Humanly speaking, it is impossible to respond to suffering with praise. But as Jesus once said to His disciples: "With man this is impossible, but with God all things are possible" (Matthew 19:26).
- "Continually"—With Jesus, it is possible to sacrifice praise "continually," through the bad times as well as the good.

This does not mean pretending to be happy when we are not. Like Freda, even through tears, we refuse to let suffering jaundice our wonder at life.

Jesus told us to expect times of suffering, and He Himself, though He was God, endured shuddering emotional, physical, and psychological pain. When times are tough and there is little in life to celebrate our worship may well mean even more to the Lord than our spontaneous expressions of gratitude in moments of easy joy. King David refused to "sacrifice to the Lord my God burnt offerings that cost me nothing" (2 Samuel 24:24).

In the long, weary, and confusing fight for my wife Samie's health, as we have clung to God and each other for dear life (literally at times), perhaps in these moments, we have been able to glorify God simply by refusing to quit. Samie's faith has often confounded me—not once in all that she has gone through have I heard her question God's love, His existence, or His lordship. As I have watched her trying to trust God in spite of unspeakable fear, hoping and holding on through so much discouragement and physical pain, I have come to the conclusion that God is glorified in suffering, too—that a life can be fully lived, to the glory of God, through pain as well as pleasure, and in fact, that such worship is the sweetest sound of all in the ears of the Lord.

Life to the full is ultimately an eternal prospect. It was Jesus Himself who said: "The man who loves his life will lose it, while the man who hates his life in this world will keep it for eternal life" (John 12:25). In this life, we may well be called to sacrifice ourselves and endure great suffering. But the Lord reminds us again and again not to get too comfortable on this side of death, but rather to store up treasures in heaven where "there will be no more death or mourning or crying or pain, for the old order of things has passed away" (Revelation 21:4).

More than a thousand years ago, the Celtic saint Columbanus pointed out that: "It is the end of the road that travelers look for and desire, and because we are travelers and pilgrims through this world, it is the road's end that we should always be thinking about." He concludes with an exhortation: "Don't let us love the road rather than the land to which it leads, lest we lose our homeland altogether."[6]

As we make Christ our vision on this long and painful journey, secure in the Father's love, as we sacrifice ourselves through many trials, so we will fulfill the vision of God and thus know fulfillment ourselves. We will be "to God the aroma of Christ … the fragrance of life" (2 Corinthians 2:15). We will live our lives fully to the eternal glory of God.

6. *Celtic Daily Prayer: Prayers and Readings from the Northumbria Community* (HarperCollins, London: 2001).

"My soul glorifies the Lord
and my spirit rejoices in God my Savior,
for he has been mindful
of the humble state of his servant.
From now on all generations will call me blessed,
for the Mighty One has done great things for me—
holy is his name."
(Mary, the mother of Jesus)

the VISION and

the Vow

GRACE

SUMMON THE LOSERS

CHAPTER FOUR
THE BAD

Last week, I was with a guy I hadn't seen for years. He's a pastor's son, and in his teens, he got a girl pregnant. I still remember the shock and shame of it all and the gracious way his parents coped. When the baby was born, the mother denied my friend access, but that was almost sixteen years ago. And any day now, that daughter of his is going to be free under British Law to contact her dad. He's massively built—formerly a construction worker and now working as a driver— but there were tears in his eyes as he told me that his teenage daughter is looking for him—she wants to find the father she has never known. There were also tears in the eyes of the wise pastor, so moved by the imminent prospect of gaining a long-lost granddaughter.

Who but God can take sin and create life and love and tears of joy from a moment of bitter sin? When we surrender our shame to Him, He removes our guilt. But He doesn't stop there; He also sets about redeeming the damage done, healing wounds and restoring relationships. This is the grace of God.

We discount ourselves from God's call to discipleship for many reasons:

- I'm too bad.
- I'm too broken.
- I'm too boring.

But ironically, the very wounds we expect to disqualify us from God's vision for our lives are often the very failures that position us to be called and used powerfully. Jesus came to seek and save the lost. He came for those who know their need of a doctor, an undertaker, or a priest. The God of the cosmos came with a target audience in mind: the poor in spirit, those who hunger and thirst for righteousness because they know they are anything but righteous right now. He came for those who are too meek to push themselves forward in the football team at school, around the water cooler at work, or when the prophet comes to town. Jesus came to heal, forgive, and commission life's greatest losers to lose even more spectacularly—for Him.

And thus, inexorably, to win.

In this chapter, we will confront the barrier of sin and the dangerous assumption that "I'm too bad" to be used by God. Then in the other chapters of this section on grace, we will address the obstacles of brokenness and self-doubt.

Judas Iscariot, perhaps the most tragic and despicable character in the whole canon of scripture, might seem at first glance to be the worst possible illustration of grace and redemption. He appears, on the evidence of the Gospels, to have had few redeeming character traits:

- He was a greedy man and a thief who exploited his position as treasurer to take money from the apostolic purse.
- He was a liar and deceiver who sank so low as to misappropriate money specifically given for the benefit of the poor.
- He was a cynical and callous schemer who carefully plotted to make sure that his betrayal was done "privately."

- He was a loner who chose a night of intimate friendship during a shared and significant meal to betray Jesus.
- He was a hard-hearted man who never accorded Jesus a higher title than "rabbi" in three years as a member of His inner core. Never once did Judas Iscariot call Jesus "Lord."

Perhaps it was inevitable that such a contemptuous character would one day betray such goodness to death. The Apostle Peter certainly seems to have thought so. In the Upper Room awaiting Pentecost, he "stood up among the believers (a group numbering about a hundred and twenty) and said, 'Brothers, the Scripture had to be fulfilled which the Holy Spirit spoke long ago through the mouth of David concerning Judas ... 'May his place be deserted; let there be no one to dwell in it,' and, 'May another take his place of leadership'" (Acts 1:15-20).

Are we therefore to assume that Judas was born on some kind of conveyor belt bound for hell? That he was predestined for death and damnation? There are plenty of people today who feel that way about themselves: "It's just the way I am." "It's my fate—it's in my astral charts." "It's the way I was brought up." "I'm a bad person, and there's nothing I can do about it." "It's a genetic compulsion." "I'm under a curse."

If Judas was under such a curse, what are we to make of the fact that Jesus chose him as one of the twelve? Twelve was significant. It was the number of the tribes of Israel. Scholars agree that Jesus was gathering a group of Israelites who could establish the new covenant, who could represent and redeem the twelve families of God's holy people—so much so that Paul would later refer to "The Twelve" when there were actually only eleven (1 Corinthians 15:5; Luke 24:33).

If Jesus chose Judas with some kind of foreknowledge that this was a man bound inexorably to betray Him and hang himself, was not the call more of a curse? And wouldn't such foreknowledge have dissuaded Jesus from choosing him as one of the twelve sons of Israel in the first place? And even if such foreknowledge did exist in King David or in Christ, is that the same as fore-ordination?

This is not the place for a theological debate about predestination; instead, I invite you to play an imagination game with me to make an important pastoral point. I invite you to consider Judas and wonder "what if?"

- What if, having betrayed Jesus to death, Judas had somehow managed to wrestle his demons a few more hours?
- What if Judas had not hanged himself that day from that tree?
- What if Judas had just held on, in living hell, for three more days on earth?

How would Judas Iscariot have responded to the resurrection of Jesus Christ?

Of course, we can never know, but we can wonder, and there are some interesting clues in scripture as to what might have happened next.

Matthew tells us that, prior to his suicide, Judas was "seized with remorse" (27:3). He ran to the priests declaring, "I have sinned, I have betrayed innocent blood," hoping there might still be some way to undo the deed. Do we dare describe these words as a confession of sin?

Judas then tried to return the blood money, flinging those thirty, dirty silver coins at the feet of the priests and fleeing in anguish. Is this repentance, or just the demented regret of a desperate man?

The priests, not wanting to be tarnished with dirty money, use the refunded coins to purchase a field as a cemetery for foreigners. And this is where—deliberately or by bitter coincidence, we cannot be sure from the biblical accounts—Judas chose to kill himself by hanging.

He had committed a sin greater than any other in the scale of its consequence. Everything seemed hopeless. What does a man think, what does he do, having betrayed the Lord to a tortured death for the price of a field? For Judas, there was no escaping the awful horror of his own heart. No future. And so, in the darkest despair, he hanged himself.

But what if he had waited a weekend? That's all that would have been needed.

I love to imagine Jesus on Easter morning deliberately seeking out the disciple more lost than any other. Perhaps now, at last, he might be found! When Judas first sees Jesus, I imagine him wondering how this tumult of madness could now be conjuring up the rabbi in his tortured mind. Slowly Jesus approaches, but Judas is frozen in disbelief. Closer. Closer. Jesus is unbearably close—so close now that Judas can feel His breath on his cheek. And then it happens: Jesus greets Judas.

With a kiss.

He is carrying three questions for Peter. He has scars to show Thomas. But first, a kiss for Judas.

And some time within those moments, I imagine two words—just two—being exchanged very quietly between the men. Jesus looks deeply into the unblinking eyes of His betrayer, who is too dumbstruck even to avert his gaze in shame. And then He utters a single syllable, upon which eternity will surely swing. Jesus whispers:

"Friend."

Do you hear the echo? It was another day, another kiss, perhaps another Judas, too. But, in the garden that night, Jesus had greeted His betrayer in just the same way. "Friend," He had said, "do what you came for." And Judas had done it, and he had not been able to undo it. And Jesus had been to hell and back as a result. And now He is standing here, impossibly, greeting Judas again, His heart unchanged for the twelfth of His disciples: "Friend." He, too, had done what He came for.

The sound of that word somehow echoes to reach Judas, lost as he is in another eternity. He hears the greeting. He feels the breath. Life to dust. Ashes to embers. A kiss for a curse. As if slowly waking from a nightmare, Judas Iscariot replies to his victim, the victor, with a single word, surely more meaningful than we can ever know:

"Lord."

It's a whisper, barely audible. And yet the sound of that word resounds like a gunshot around the halls of heaven. "Lord." The angels gasp in recognition: "Not rabbi—Lord! Even Judas, even Judas," they say.

And then perhaps Judas, in those awkward, awestruck moments, moves to reciprocate the kiss, as one should. Should he? Could he? Would Jesus allow it once again?

And as his lips touch the cheek, it is as though a pin pierces his stupor—his body just crumples upon Christ's, shuddering with the greatest sobs of redemption in human history. Somehow the irreversible sin has become the very door to salvation—even for him, the twelfth, the last, the least, the thief, the greatest traitor of them all.

With those tears, the angelic realm erupts in praise. "Rejoice with me," cries the Spirit, His voice echoing through heaven, "for I have found my lost sheep!" and there is always "more rejoicing in heaven over one sinner who repents than over ninety-nine righteous persons who do not need to repent" (Luke 15:6). Praises ring to the Lamb that was slain for the sins of the world—even this, the greatest sin of them all. Truly He loves His enemy and does good to His persecutor. He is the shepherd who left the eleven to find at last His one lost sheep. He is the Alpha and Omega who takes the twelfth brother and makes him first, lifting his name as the ultimate example of grace—insurmountable and eternal proof of the power of love to conquer sin.

I imagine the hesitant reconciliation between Judas and the eleven comrades he had also betrayed later that day. Peter, of course, vents his anger at the very sight of Judas, but it soon passes like a storm. Gentle John is more complicated, but when he hears Judas naming Jesus, "Lord," his loyal heart melts in forgiveness.

Some days later, I imagine Judas there with the others in the Upper Room on the day of Pentecost, and he, too, is being filled with the Holy Spirit now, just as surely as Satan had entered into him back then at the Last Supper.

And then, some years after his Great Commission, I imagine Judas dying a martyr's death in some far-flung corner of the world—not hanging hopelessly from that tree—but standing valiantly for the one he calls Lord.

I imagine the message of hope the Apostle Judas might have brought to millions down the years who felt their sin was too bad, their situation impossible, their guilt irreversible, their self-loathing immeasurable.

And I imagine him in heaven, perhaps between David the adulterer and Paul the murderer, singing with joy beyond measure:

> *"Amazing grace, how sweet the sound,*
> *that saved a wretch like me ..."*

51

Yes, I believe there was even grace for Judas, if only he could have held on through that one dark and desperate weekend.

But of course, his guilt appeared too great, and so he hanged himself, and his belly split open, as though (to quote Augustine) the violence of his crime was just too great for a human body to contain. And when he hanged himself, perhaps grace was robbed by a mere three days of one of the greatest testimonies of all time.

Please do not despair of grace. Never give up. Resist the temptation to pass judgment on yourself like Judas—that is the path of madness and self-destruction. No matter how desperate you may feel today, hold on for tomorrow. Stumble on a few more hours in blind faith, offering God nothing more than your hopelessness and your sin. We cannot rush the resurrection. But wait and watch, and He will surely come.

No matter what you have done, I am convinced of this: There is more grace in God than sin in you. I defy you to tempt such love with so much as a breath or a glance or a whisper of confession. Just one prodigal pace is all it takes to bring your Father running to greet you with the kiss of His grace.

And He will call you "friend."

And you will call Him "Lord."

CHAPTER FIVE
THE BROKEN

A young and relatively unknown actor called Mark Hamill had been delighted to land the part of Luke Skywalker in the first *Star Wars* movie. Of course, the film went on to exceed every possible expectation of success, and Hamill enthusiastically accepted the invitation to return as Skywalker in *The Empire Strikes Back*, despite a prior commitment to play a part in a low-grade TV series, due to be filmed around the same time. The producers of the TV show refused to release Hamill from his contract, confident that his presence would boost their ratings—especially if the *Star Wars* sequel should happen to do as well as the original.

Legend has it that, just days before filming was due to begin, Mark was involved in a car crash which left him with a broken nose and a scar on his face. The TV company—having no use for a disfigured star—quickly released Hamill from his contract. But George Lucas' response was different: Seeing that his baby-faced hero was now scarred and bruised, he re-wrote the opening scenes of the film. And that is why *The Empire Strikes Back* begins with Luke Skywalker not in a jungle as originally scripted, but trudging through snow—his face covered up because of the cold—until he encounters a terrible snow-monster. The hideous beast strikes him across the face, leaving Luke scarred for the rest of the film. George Lucas had taken a disaster and used it to make the film better.[1]

So many of us are disfigured by life, and we assume God will respond to us

---

1. Thanks to Winkie Pratney who uses this illustration.

like the fast-buck TV company, by rejecting us for our imperfections—cutting us out of its plans. But in fact, like George Lucas carefully creating his masterpiece around Hamill's scars, the Creator takes the wounds of our lives and uses them to make an even better story. The Bible calls this redemption. God does not reject us for our scars, and He does more than merely *rescue* us from our pain. God *redeems* our lives. He turns weakness into strength, ugliness into beauty, and weaves the scars of sin and pain into an even better story. Through David's adultery, God gave us the beauty and comfort of Psalm 51. Through the treachery of Judas, we are saved. Through a broken body on a cross, grace makes us whole.

THE MOVIE OF OUR LIVES

One of my best friends, John, was beaten and abused throughout his childhood by his stepfather. As a teenager, he found himself drawn into addictive and self-destructive patterns of behavior, and then as a student deep in the drug scene, he came close to a lethal overdose. The damage done to John by this history of abuse and rejection has been profound, and I refuse to trivialize his experiences into some trite point about God's happy healing. The truth is that even now, as a grown man with a responsible job and a vibrant Christian faith, John still struggles most days with a subtle sense of rejection and puzzles over the meaning of God's unconditional love for him.

But on his journey into wholeness, John often startles me with deep insights into God's love that I could never have seen without him. From his brokenness comes a unique understanding of God and a convincing testament to grace. The movie of John's life really is worth watching—it is blemished, funny, painful, and profound, because the Director has not airbrushed the imperfections away from John's features, nor has He re-cast the part in search of eye-candy. Instead, the wounds and the scars of John's life add depth to his character and make the story even better; they are being redeemed.

Whenever—to quote Isaiah—the mourning of the broken-hearted becomes gladness and such despair is turned to praise, God is glorified by a life fully lived against the odds—a particularly beautiful "display of his splendor" (Isaiah 61).

THE LETTER OF OUR LIVES

The brilliant German poet Rainer Maria Rilke was born in Prague on an icy December day in 1875. His mother was evidently still grieving the tragic death of her first-born daughter, because she transferred the anguish of her broken heart onto her newborn son in many bizarre ways. Until the age of six, she pretended he was a girl, dressing him, as he later confessed, "like a big doll." She was a religious woman and would take Rilke as an infant to pray for hours in churches and even to kiss Christ's wounds on the crucifix.

Meanwhile, Rilke's father was an austere, uncommunicative figure who had been a cadet in the emperor's army. At age ten, Rilke was sent away to military school, where in a single day, his unusually and confusingly feminine childhood turned into a hyper-masculine, regimented, and cruel adolescence. He was bullied, misunderstood, and terribly lonely, finding refuge only in the school infirmary.

In such a hostile world, too male for his mother and too sensitive for such a school, Rilke developed a passion for poetry, channelling his brokenness into something beautiful. Thus the very circumstances that might so easily have been the breaking of the man instead became the making of him. Rilke went to university, where he became one of the wild young things of his day, dressing flamboyantly for the times (with silver-headed cane and bowler hat) and throwing himself into relationships. By now, he knew that he had been put on earth to be a poet, and when few others believed in his ability, he was undaunted, publishing his own work, handing it out in the streets free of charge, and writing bold letters to the great literary figures of his day.

Despite understandable family pressures to take some more respectable route through life, Rilke's artistic vision meant more to him than money, more to him than status, and even more to him than his family. At any cost, he was determined to be true to himself and to the heartbeat of his call. Rainer Maria Rilke wrote about life, about poverty, about death, and especially about God, and although he lived out his days in relative obscurity, his brokenness continues to touch the world with an unusual beauty.

In one of his poems, Rilke offers an heroic depiction of Michelangelo:

> *That was a man beyond measure—a giant—*
> *who forgot what the immeasurable was.*
> *He was the kind of man who turns*
> *to bring forth the meaning of an age*
> *that wants to end.*
> *He lifts its whole weight*
> *and heaves it into the chasm of his heart.*[2]

Michelangelo, Van Gogh, Dylan Thomas, Kurt Cobain, Rilke—such artists may appear on the canvas of history as men "beyond measure—giants." But the briefest exploration of their actual lives reveals the underlying truth that they were in fact broken, needy people touched by grace.

Rilke, no doubt reflecting on the pain of his own life and the pressure to submit meekly to the expectations of his parents, visualized a letter hidden inside every person at birth (we might call it destiny or God's call). Only if we are true to ourselves, he said, may we open the envelope and read the letter of our lives before we die. When life leaves us broken, the natural tendency is to shrink our horizons and hide in the crowd. As a result, many people go to their graves without ever reading the letter of their lives. Rilke himself could so easily have been suppressed

2. "Das Waren Tage Michelangelo's," Anita Barrows and Joanna Macy, *Rilke's Book of Hours* (Riverhead Books, New York, NY: 1996) p. 71.

and oppressed by the pain of his childhood, but instead, he turned the pain into passion and resolutely pronounced every syllable of the letter of his life for the joy of many. In one of his most poignant poems, W.H. Auden takes Rilke's idea one step further with these challenging words:

> *God may reduce you*
> *on Judgment Day*
> *To tears of shame,*
> *reciting by heart*
> *The poems you would*
> *have written, had*
> *Your life been good.*[3]

ANNA

The prophetess Anna in the Bible read the letter and wrote the poem of her life to the glory of God. She wasn't always a prophetess, and personally, I don't think she was automatically destined to be featured in the pages of scripture either. At one time, she was just another happily married housewife, blending in perfectly with the others in her street. And then, after just seven years of marriage, her husband died—we don't know how—and she faced the biggest trial of her life. Without warning, the young woman's world was invaded by tragedy; her dreams lay shattered about her feet. Widowed and childless, she must have considered the future bleak indeed. But Anna turned her pain into persevering passion; she dedicated herself unceasingly to prayer and worship in the temple. And so, at least sixty years later, we find the irrepressible Anna, now eighty-four years old, holding the baby Jesus in her arms, arms that had never held a child of their own, and she is thanking Jehovah with all her heart, prophesying over the very Son of God.

Here is a woman who, in spite of her pain (or perhaps because of it), resolutely

---

3. W.H. Auden, *Thanksgiving for a Habitat, Collected Poems*, Edward Mendelson ed. (Random House, New York, NY: 1976) p. 525.

read the letter of her life. As a young woman, she could easily and understandably have turned inwards to become bitter and frightened, never again to give herself to others and never again to truly trust God. She might easily have echoed the sad conclusion of Job: "My days have passed, my plans are shattered, and so are the desires of my heart" (17: 11). But instead, she began to re-imagine the ruins of her life, discovering a new vision that would one day even herald the coming of Christ. Anna delighted herself in the Lord, and she received the desires of her heart (Psalm 37:4).

As Christians, our vision is not just some existential aspiration of self-improvement through positive thought. Our vision is "dangerously, obsessively, undeniably Jesus." And as we surrender our lives for Christ, we find them. As we seek first the kingdom, we discover that "all things" are given to us. As we stop obsessing about our own destiny and reputation and simply seek to live for Jesus' sake, we read the letter of our lives. And it is funny and sad and written in blood, more precious than words. In losing our lives for Christ, we inherit the world itself.

58

The Creator comes to each one of us as He came to Rilke and as He came to Anna. He grants us a number of breaths, a number of beats of the heart, in which to make a little history through prayer, through pain, and with such resilient imagination that each passing moment, each New Year's Eve, may become an "amen" to the words of His Son, who came "that they may have life, and have it to the full" (John 10:10).

CHAPTER SIX
THE BORING

few years ago, a bitter dispute broke out about who had the world's longest ear hair. The *Guinness Book of Records* announced that the title belonged to an Indian gentleman by the name of B.D. Tyagi, whose aural strands at the time extended a luxuriant four inches (10.2 cm.). But then a farmer—one Narayan Prasad Pal from Orissa State—indignantly laid claim to the record, having cultivated two truly remarkable wisps of hair, each one a full five inches long. "I am proud of my hair. I want to have the record until I die," he told the world's media, concluding with this poignant admission: "Other than this, I have not achieved much in life."

He stood there, sixty-five years old, looking back on his life. I imagine him holding those incomparable strands of ear hair out horizontally on each side of his head as though a piece of twine was passing in one ear and out the other: "Other than this," he says to the gathered journalists, as he gently twiddles the strands, "I have not achieved much in life." It's a confession both funny and tragic.

People go to extreme lengths (excuse the pun) to rise above mediocrity, while others resign themselves to achieving little in life.

When it comes to God's vision for our lives, I suspect that the greatest obstacle to grace for most people is not some cycle of heinous sin, nor the razor-shards of brokenness. I suspect that the greatest source of spiritual inertia for most of us is merely a dreary sense of personal mediocrity.

The dramatic testimonies of the bad and the broken can make our ordinary lives seem mind-numbingly boring by comparison. We know with absolute certainty that Jesus can do amazing things for satanists, drug dealers, gun runners, C-list celebrities, and anorexic ballerinas, but it's hard to imagine Him intervening dramatically in lesser lives that are not so much desperate as just plain dull. And so we sit in our sycamore trees to catch a glimpse of Jesus, and never in our wildest dreams (which aren't very wild at all) do we expect Him to notice people like us, let alone single us out for a chat and an invitation to tea.

"Until a man is nothing, God can make nothing out of him."
(Martin Luther)

Let me tell you a story about a man who lived his whole life quite convinced that he was a nobody—the kind of guy who sometimes wonders if God has passed him by and would quite understand it if He did. You won't have heard of him (of course), but his name was Brian. To my brothers and me, he was simply Dad.

The first thing to say is that my father was two years older than my grandfather. Most people can't figure that statement out at first, but it's true! Dad married late, and as a result, he was thirty years older than his wife, my mother, and a couple of years older than her father. Because of his age, Dad was often tired and ill, but he was also warm, kind, humble, and understated, with the timeless reserve of an English gentleman. He wore a tie in the summer, called people "old boy," and had his shoes repaired by a cobbler in town. To this day, when I hear the steady clip, clip, clip of metal-heeled shoes on the road, I remember a square-shouldered, gray-haired man with laughter lines crinkling out from hazel eyes. His vast hands, with veins like a road map, are clasped behind his back, and without warning, the word "Dad" thuds in my heart. That was my father, and one day, you may meet him and love him, too.

He went to Oxford University to read the classics in the years between the wars, and there he met Jimmy Cox. Jimmy had a wonderful presence about him, and as the men became friends, Dad discovered that it was the presence of Jesus.

Much to the consternation of his parents, Dad became a Christian, too, and proceeded to lead his brother, my uncle, to Jesus as well. After graduation, he joined the family law firm in London as expected, but in his heart, something was stirring—a sense that God was calling him to Brazil as a missionary.

The prospect appeared to have terrified him as he wrestled with the growing conviction that God might indeed be asking him to leave his sheltered existence working for the family firm to become a pioneer evangelist in an unreached tribe. "I feel absolutely unfit for this work in Brazil," he wrote on one of many scraps of paper, on which he also confessed to feeling "unfit for the task," to lacking any real love toward God "and the men for whom He died," and to having a "weak character."

61

However, still feeling quite certain that he was too ordinary to be used by God in such an extraordinary way, my Dad made his decision. He left the office, defied the wishes of his father, abandoned the soft comforts of home, quit the city, swapping his briefcase for a suitcase, and made his way to missionary training college to prepare himself for service in the Brazilian interior. He had finally found the courage to step off the conveyor belt, to face up to the potent disapproval of his father, and to set out on his own adventure with God, come what may. This was it: his big opportunity to be somebody significant and to do something extraordinary with his life for God.

HERO TO ZERO

Then, several months into Dad's missionary training, his disapproving father suffered a heart attack. Word came quickly: My grandfather was alive, but needed his son in London. Sensing that this was a call from his heavenly Father as well as a summons from home, Dad dutifully made his way back to the drudgery of an office. It was in some ways the death of a dream.

Going to Brazil had been his big break—the chance of a lifetime—and suddenly it had all been shattered by a dreary call to return to the monotone world of London, there to do his mundane duty, running the family firm and nursing a man who had never wanted him to leave in the first place.

Dad felt that in Brazil, his life might have amounted to something—perhaps he could even have been a Jimmy Cox for some primitive Amazonian tribesman. At least he might somehow have made a mark on the world with his sacrificial adventure. In Brazil, he would have been a somebody. Commenting later he said, "I had to learn to be a nobody and go nowhere before God could use me."

And so he did his duty. Worked hard as a solicitor. Cared for his parents until they died. He organized Bible studies in the city and supported frontline missionaries from behind the scenes. He liked sports, but he never excelled at them. He had passed his law exams, but only on the second attempt. He married, but very late. During the war, he was conscripted as an officer in the RAF, but while Jimmy Cox died a hero's death in The Battle of Britain, Dad fought a quiet war doing administration half a world away from the frontline.

And he loved people. He became a very good lawyer, but never really made any money from it because he didn't like charging clients if he knew they couldn't afford it. As a result, all sorts of needy people would appear at his office door, and our childhood was filled with eccentric and exotic characters befriended by my father as he went beyond the call of any legal duty.

- There was a rather glamorous Swiss woman who had somehow managed to marry a satanist and telephoned screaming one night to say that he was trying to kill her and could she come to stay.

- There was Josephine, a bird-like Austrian-Jewess who had fled Hitler and now lived in England in a little apartment surrounded by junk in plastic bags. She terrified my brothers and me, but had been hired as our piano teacher because—as I later realized—Dad wanted to give her work.
- There was the frightened little Cockney lady so neurotic about life that Dad promptly hired her as his trusted secretary and invited her to join us for Christmas.
- There were dignitaries, like one former mayor of Kensington who had lost a finger when an African tribesman went berserk with a machete. As kids, we were all simply terrified of shaking his hand.

And so my dear old dad lived out his life faithfully. In his latter years, he fought depression and the cruel deterioration of age, no longer able to give as much as he once had and often feeling like a failure.

Then my father died.

In the dark days following his departure, a small avalanche of letters confirmed what we had suspected all along: that there had never been anything ordinary about Dad at all, that countless lives had been changed forever by his unassuming example. A commander in the Royal Navy wrote to say that Dad had been "the best friend any man could have." Several letters said that his unassuming kindness had been a critical factor in leading them to faith in Christ, and one of these testimonies came from the father of a famous evangelist. Meanwhile, an old friend, who was not a Christian, described Dad as "the finest and truest man I know." I wonder how many of life's high achievers will ever deserve such a plaudit.

This man, so convinced that he had been called to be nobody special, was in fact somebody extraordinary for countless people in every walk of life. He visited the sick, took on clients whom he knew could or would never pay him, and witnessed quietly to many about his faith.

THE ADVENTURE OF NORMAL

In people like my dad, and thousands of faceless heroes like him, we see that there is no such thing as a small life.

There is an adventure before us, and God has chosen us precisely because of our sense of inadequacy: "Isn't it obvious," Paul asks, "that God deliberately chose men and women that the culture overlooks and exploits and abuses, chose these 'nobodies' to expose the hollow pretensions of the 'somebodies'?" (1 Corinthians 1:27-28 MSG).

64

Everything Dad taught me was by example and not by rote. I picture him now, through the crack in the door, kneeling by his bed each night, those big hands clasped in silent prayer. I cannot be sure what inner sighs and backward glances he brought before his Father, kneeling there each night. But of this I am certain: that God sometimes replied, "Well done, my son. Well done, my good and faithful servant. Well done, my humble friend."

The world is full of anonymous heroes—nobody-somebodies—like Brian Greig. Sometimes God chooses such ordinary people to do extraordinary things, as He did with Gideon. But more often, He uses ordinary people to do ordinary things with extraordinary kindness. This is a form of heroism that Hollywood does not understand, the type of visionary ignored by history. Such faithful servants "don't need fame from names," but live out their days in quiet humility, unrecognized by human applause. Yet perhaps these will be the real heroes of heaven: the meek, the merciful, and the poor in spirit blessed by God, the humble ones He has lovingly exalted.

HIGH ACHIEVERS

When Jesus was baptized, the heavens opened, and His Father spoke, saying, "This is my Son, whom I love; with him I am well pleased." What an incredible moment! But let us remember that, at this point in Jesus' life, He hadn't actually done anything publicly. His open ministry hadn't begun. For thirty years, he had simply lived a normal life in a nowhere town with quiet integrity, growing "in wisdom and stature, and in favor with God and men" (Luke 2:52). The affirmation of the Father had come to Him before His ministry ever began.

My three-year-old son Daniel often brings his paintings home from nursery school. We love them because we love him, and Samie puts them straight on the fridge door. I have never heard her criticizing his lack of perspective, his unrealistic use of color, or his poor technique. She doesn't wait for his work to match that of Leonardo da Vinci or Vincent Van Gogh before thanking him. In fact, Danny's scribbles and dribbles of color touch Samie's heart in a way that the great works of the maestros never could.

65

Too often we feel like failures, comparing ourselves unfavorably with those who seem more skilled—a better catch for Christ. But whatever we do for God and truly give to Him—the scribbles and dribbles of an average life—takes pride of place on our heavenly Father's fridge door.

No one is too boring, too broken, or too bad to be called, commissioned, and used significantly by God. We are eternally precious souls for whom Christ Himself died, which means that the stakes are too high for easy excuses of inadequacy. Nelson Mandela said: "Your playing small doesn't serve the world."[1] The Apostle Paul said that "Christ in you [is] the hope of glory" (Colossians 1:27). And C.S. Lewis, in his beautiful book *The Weight of Glory*, defied us to settle for anything less:

"There are no ordinary people. You have never met a mere mortal. Nations, cultures, arts, civilizations—these are mortal and their life is to ours as a gnat.

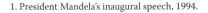

1. President Mandela's inaugural speech, 1994.

But it is immortals whom we joke with, work with, marry, snub, and exploit—immortal horrors or everlasting splendors."[2]

2. *The Weight of Glory*, C.S. Lewis—Commemoration of Charles Williams, 1945.

the Vow

the VISION and

DISCIPLESHIP

THE ARMY IS DISCIPL(IN)ED

"Then Jesus said to his disciples,
'If anyone would come after me,
he must deny himself and take up his cross and follow me.
For whoever wants to save his life will lose it,
but whoever loses his life for me will find it.'"
(Matthew 16:24-25)

CHAPTER SEVEN
WHEN JESUS SAYS "COME"

*"I have a vision,
I have a vision ...
television!"
(Bono, U2 Zoo Tour)*

The word "tele-vision" literally describes a vision that is "far off" or distant. Gazing mesmerized at that screen night after night, we experience life, but we do so vicariously, second-hand, one step removed from reality. We watch documentaries about other peoples' discoveries, soap operas about imaginary communities. Even the news programs amount to little more than the perspectives of others about what is important in the world.

Of course, television is not intrinsically wrong. It can be a brilliant window to the world. And we all need an evening of escapism once in a while. But we must beware of living secondhand lives through the screens of make believe. It's just too easy to be entertained by TV, DVD, or VDU at the expense of conversation, community, and the chaotic immediacy of real life. Exhilarating words like "Adventure," "Comedy," and "Romance" get reduced to mere genres of entertainment in the video store. Our vision becomes "far-off."

In sharp contrast to television reality, Christ's vision for our lives is always immediate—never "far-off":

- "Pick up your mat."
- "Sell everything you have and give to the poor."
- "Come let us go for the hour is near."

Jesus walks (a relative stranger) into your living room while you're watching the news. He looks at you, winks, and indicates the television: "I'll take you there. Come with me!" Suddenly, it dawns on you that you've been bored for longer than you can remember, and something seems to wake up inside—the part of you that remembers how it feels to fall in love and still gets scared of the dark and one day wants more than anything else to scream so loud that a window really breaks.

And so, without a word, you stand, switch off the "far-off" vision in the corner, and follow the relative stranger out through your own front door.

When the relative stranger presented Himself on the stony shores of Galilee and called His first disciples to leave their nets and come, it was—of course—a life-changing invitation. Without warning, all the "far-off" dreams and patient prayers for a messiah, or a prophet, or a sign, imploded into a single, simple challenge: "Come ..."

Those faithful sons of Abraham, busy pulling fish from a lake, suddenly found an ordinary working day hijacked by the immediate and eternal. Without a second thought, they obeyed. Left their nets. Followed. Never stopped.

Discipleship would not have been a strange concept for Simon, James, John, and the rest. Every tradition had its trainees: The disciples of Moses who diligently studied the Mosaic Law; the disciples of the Pharisees, pillars of the community seeking to understand and apply the Torah and the oral traditions of their Fathers. And then there was John the Baptizer's radical band of disciples, too.

It was a great honor to be accepted as a disciple in such groups, and the prospects for anyone apprenticed to a reputed rabbi were good. During the period of study, the disciple would resign himself—like students down the ages—to relative poverty and a season of hard work. But once he had "graduated," he would be a rabbi—a position of high social standing with its own financial rewards.

Membership of these rabbinical schools was so desirable that the rabbis would never have needed to "recruit" disciples. Instead, hopeful students would come to them hoping to be accepted into the group. The first surprise, therefore, for those Jesus chose was the very fact that He approached them! "You did not choose me," Jesus reminds them three years later, "but I chose you ..." (John 15:16).

POP IDOL

In our celebrity-obsessed world, *Idol* is aptly named. In the minds of millions, it is the ultimate accolade to be chosen by an arrogant panel of judges and a frantic flurry of thirteen year olds voting by SMS to win the prize of fame, fortune, and a record contract.

How much more wonderful to be chosen by Jesus to receive a divine call—a mind-blowing kindness, the supreme honor. Obedience to such a call is not a favor to the Almighty, nor is it a lifestyle choice to be picked up and put down at will. "It is only when we begin to see ourselves as chosen, called and commissioned by Christ," wrote David Watson, "that we shall have any real sense of our responsibility to present our bodies to him 'as a living sacrifice, holy and acceptable to God.'"

73

I was giving a friend a lift in my car, and we got to talking about life. "I don't know what God's calling me to do," he confessed, and asked me to pray about what it might be.

"Why?" I asked. "I already know what Jesus wants you to do!"

"You do?" he gasped with excitement. "So, what is it? What's my call?"

I paused, enjoying the suspense. Drums rolled. String quartets tuned up. My friend held his breath ...

"Your call," I said slowly, "is to be a worship leader ..."

He looked pleased, really pleased, so I continued: "... but not necessarily with a guitar in your hand."

"Okayyy," he murmured.

"Your call is to befriend that funny little lady at the end of your street ..."

He seemed less pleased with this prospect.

"Your call is to feed the hungry and to spend yourself on behalf of the poor ..."

By now he was looking distinctly troubled.

"... and to offer hospitality to strangers who just turn up in town needing a place to crash."

Consternation.

"And it's to fast."

74

He was starting to look furious.

"And it's to pray so long and hard that you run out of words and tears."

There was no going back:

"Your call," I continued, "is to preach the good news of Jesus to every person who will listen and a few who won't. Your call is to go somewhere, anywhere, wherever, whenever, for Jesus, and never stop. Your call is to love people no one else loves and to forgive them when they treat you like dirt—or worse. Do your job to the very best of your ability without grumbling about your boss or whining about your colleagues. Your call is to pray for the sick, and when they are healed, to dance all night. And when they aren't, to weep with them and love them even more."

I glanced across at him and was relieved to see that his expression was beginning to mellow.

"Your call is to honor your parents, pray for your leaders, study the Scriptures, and attend plenty of parties. Be a peacemaker in every situation: when the fight breaks out on the bus home late at night and when the gossip starts to circulate at church. Your call is to pick up litter in the street when no one else is looking, to wipe the toilet seat, to pull the gum off from under the desk. It's to get to meetings early to put out the chairs."

By now he was smiling.

"Your call is to make disciples and to teach them to obey everything Jesus commanded. And don't forget to minister grace to them when they sin. Which they will. Your mission is to baptize and to cast out evil spirits. Your call is to bind up broken hearts wherever you find them, and you will find them wherever you look. It's to visit prisons. And hospitals. And to ..."

"Yeah, yeah," he interrupted good naturedly, trying to shut me up, but I was on a roll—and I knew he couldn't leave, because I was driving the car.

"Your call," I continued resolutely, "is to listen more than you talk and to listen with your eyes as well as your ears."

He was shaking his head in mock despair. I carried on: "It's to do the chores again and again without grumbling. It's to buy ethical coffee and to recycle your bottles. And while you're at it, don't forget to leave anonymous gifts on people's doorsteps."

By now we were both laughing, and I was finally running out of steam: "And when you've done all that," I grinned, jabbing him in the ribs at each syllable, "come back and see me, and we can spend a little time praying about Phase Two!"

The problem for most of us is not that we don't know what God wants of us. It's that we know exactly what He wants of us, and it's not what we want to do!

When Samie calls the kids to switch off the TV and come for dinner, they generally don't hear until at least the third time of asking. But in our house, there appears to be a mysterious acoustical phenomenon whereby the call to come for ice cream, issued in a quieter voice, carries down the hallway so that the kids hear immediately and come running right away.

General William Booth, founder of the Salvation Army, once turned to a young man who claimed not to have had a call from God. "What?" he bellowed, fixing him with his piercing eyes: "You've never *had* a call? You mean you've never *heard* the call!"

Christ's call to discipleship is written large on every single page of the New Testament. We are quick—like my kids who come running for ice-cream—to respond to His offer of love, healing, forgiveness, significance, and friendship, but slow to hear His call to do the things we do not want to do—big or small—and to go to the places and people we would rather avoid. We know Jesus as Friend, we trust Him as Savior, but only reluctantly do we obey Him as Lord.

Back on the shores of Galilee, Andrew and Simon had abandoned their nets excitedly, accepting the unexpected invitation to join Jesus' fledgling rabbinic school. As ensuing weeks unfolded, the brothers often had cause to look back on their decision to quit commercial fishing with the warm certainty of men who knew they'd made a great decision.

It is fascinating to watch the way Jesus gently led His disciples and nurtured their growth in grace. He never expected them to jump to the top of the staircase in one go, but guided them gently but firmly to the next level of sacrifice one step at a time. "I have much more to say to you," he admitted on one occasion, "more than you can now bear" (John 16:12).

There seems to be a cycle at work in Christ's discipling process, as recorded in the Gospels, which may be summarized as:

- See.
- Sacrifice.
- Celebrate.[1]

---

1. There are many helpful models of change developed by psychologists to describe the way people's behaviors are transformed. This *See-Sacrifice-Celebrate* model is a highly simplified adaptation of the most famous and widely accepted model: Prochaska and DiClemente's *Cycle of Change* traces behavioral change through four stages of pre-contemplation, contemplation, action, and maintenance.

First the disciples were allowed to *see* something significant—they received revelation about some wonderful new dimension of God's purposes that surprised them and inspired them to respond.

Then came the *sacrifice*—the cost of engagement, the practical challenge without which they could not proceed.

After sacrifice came *celebration*—having come through the previous trials, they could experience the blessing of God.

The celebration phase then either coincides with or precedes the next level of revelation, and the cycle begins again. This pattern is reflected in the chronology of all four Gospels. For instance, let's look at Matthew's account:

See: An invitation to join the rabbinic school of Jesus: "Come follow me!" (Matthew 4).

Sacrifice: To follow, they must leave their nets and families (Matthew 4).

Celebrate: The crowds, the teaching, the miracles—this is exciting! (Matthew 5-8).

See: Jesus walks on water, and they worship: "Truly you are the Son of God" (Matthew 14). Peter's confession: "You are the Christ" (Matthew 16). The transfiguration (Matthew 17).

Sacrifice: *Crises of confidence:* Disciples "filled with grief" (Matthew 7:23). "We have left everything to follow you! What then will there be for us?" (Matthew 19:27). *Crises of competence:* Failure to heal a boy with a demon (Matthew 17). Struggles for position (Matthew 18, 20).

Celebrate: Triumphal entry into Jerusalem (Matthew 21).

See: Crowds cheering "Hosanna!" (Matthew 21:1-11). "If you believe, you will receive whatever you ask for in prayer" (Matthew 21:21). Show-downs with the religious authorities.

Sacrifice: *Crises of commission:* "You are not to be called 'Rabbi'" (Matthew 23:8)—kill the idea of your own rabbinic school here and now! The temple will be destroyed—your only religious compass is to be me. Apocalyptic warnings (Matthew 24). I will depart, but you will find me in the poor (Matthew 25).

Celebrate: Passover meal (Matthew 26).

Many times on their three-year journey with Jesus, the disciples passed through this cycle of discovery, obedience, and joy, and as they did so, their relationship with Him evolved, and they were changed. When they were first called to follow, they had done so as enthusiastic students apprenticed to a rabbi. But as they began to realize that He was more than a rabbi, their identity shifted to that of servants, submitting themselves to one far greater than themselves.

And then, at a pivotal moment prior to His passion, Jesus redefines the nature of the relationship once again. "I no longer call you servants," He says (implying that He had previously). "Instead, I have called you friends, for everything that I learned from my Father I have made known to you" (John 15:15).

It is possible to break the *see-sacrifice-celebrate* cycle at any point and stall the process of transformation.

1. Some people never even get to the "see" stage, either because they have never heard the good news about Jesus or because they are too hard-hearted to believe (i.e., Caiaphas).

2. Some people see the wonders of God, but they are unwilling to pay the price and make the sacrifices He requires (i.e., the Rich Young Ruler). Entire churches can get locked at this stage of development. They receive some wonderful revelation from God, but

never move forward in obedience. As a result the community stagnates, and the revelation that once energized them grows stale.

3. Some people make wonderful sacrifices for Jesus, but they never move on to celebrate His blessing. This can be because they are unable to accept blessing and joy from God's hand—only hardship and challenge (this condition is more common than we might at first realize). The other reason people may fail to move from sacrifice to celebration is that they may feel resentful about the price they have paid. I once knew a woman who felt "led" to give a very large amount of her inheritance away. But, having done so, she failed to live in the joy of her own generosity and instead lived for years with a sense of bitter regret. She had sacrificed, but was never able to celebrate, and it would have been better if she had never given in the first place.

4. Many people do not move beyond celebration back into fresh revelation. They rest on past glories, recounting old stories of revelation and personal sacrifice, locked in a single cycle of discipleship, but never moving on to the next season of discovery and discipleship. As a result, they stop journeying and growing in their faith.

With the exception of Judas, Jesus' disciples continued on the cycles of discipleship (through many failures) and were transformed in the process into amazing people, world-changing visionaries, and worthy ambassadors of heaven. They had begun the journey as students, but as their understanding of Christ enlarged, they had become His servants and ultimately His friends, willing to lay down their lives in sacrificial love.

In my late teens, I went through a phase of great intensity, beating myself up with questions like:

- Am I willing to be martyred?
- How can I justify spending money on a new stereo when that money could save someone's life in the developing world?
- If Jesus is not Lord of all, is He really my Lord at all?

Around this time, I preached to my friends in graphic terms about the unspeakable agony Jesus suffered on the cross, concluding with a challenge to follow in His footsteps. I realize now that, while these are all legitimate challenges, I had much to learn about grace. Jesus challenged His disciples by degrees as they grew in their understanding and ability to respond. He always revealed His love before He appealed for sacrifice; He awaited hunger and never force-fed them with the meat of maturity.

Samie and I met on a year-long training program run by the Pioneer network of churches in the U.K. I had just graduated from university in London and had shaggy fair hair and a pretty decent tan and wore a biker's jacket with a pair of baggy dungarees (which weren't nearly as cool back then as you might suppose). The overall effect earned me the nickname "Huck" (as in, Huckleberry Fin) and doubtless plenty of less charitable monikers behind my back. Samie had long blond hair, big blue eyes, a wardrobe full of baggy jumpers and leggings, which actually were cool back then, and a playful sense of fun that always gathered a small crowd to her side. She also had a car.

We were put together in a team of six for a year, during which the chemistry between us was undeniable. Only we both denied it. Adamantly.

On one of our first free days, Samie and I drove over two hundred miles "just for fun," to drink tea in the scenic English Lake District. Driving home down winding country lanes under the stars that night, we even (and I really dread admitting this to you) listened to a song by the Carpenters and *sang along*, which is the clearest sign known to man that a guy has taken leave of his senses and has taken up a position *on the top of the world looking down on creation* ... (as the song begins).

For everyone observing my behavior, *the only explanation they could find* was the *love that I'd found ever since she'd been around* (as the song continues). Samie and I were unable to admit such feelings because we had been forbidden from indulging in "exclusive relationships" for the duration of our discipleship course. This ban to which we were sworn was affectionately known as "Section Six." How happily we had committed ourselves to this heady ideal, and how hellish the reality now seemed.

81

SECTION SIX

My desire to listen to the Carpenters was a dire symptom of a sickness that could no longer be denied. I was in love.

I immediately confessed this catastrophe to my mentor, Roger, who advised me "not to wear my heart on my sleeve" and took me to see his fish-breeding program. From that day onwards, I determined to keep my heart firmly fixed in its proper place behind the pouch of my dungarees. I also obediently abandoned Karen Carpenter on top of her mountain to resume moshing in the pit with indie bands.

But Samie was perplexed. Unknown to me, she felt the same way and had also decided to confess to her mentor, Margaret, about the feelings she had for the guy with the sad—make that maniacally depressed—wardrobe. I was ignoring Samie, keeping my heart as far as possible from my sleeve, but Samie simply concluded that she must have done something terrible to upset me. And so she asked me what it was ...

I said she hadn't done anything wrong, and so she asked me why I was ignoring her. I just couldn't think how to reply without a lie, and it all suddenly seemed so stupid anyway to keep pretending, and so I heard myself mumbling something embarrassing about "fancying her."

Samie then told me that the feeling was mutual. The earth stopped. Trumpets sounded. And we wondered what to do next. Without the iron rule of Section Six, I guess, we might have kissed. Or at least hummed a short Carpenters medley. But instead, bewildered at finding our hearts illicitly stapled to our cuffs and flapping around for all to see, we ran in opposite directions like repelling magnets to confess non-existent sins to our respective mentors.

Roger seemed to take it all very seriously indeed, except that he kept grinning. So we ended up feeding his fish. Samie, on the other hand, was having a bewildering encounter with her mentor.

"Why don't you just go out with him?" Margaret asked, without any warning whatsoever.

This was not in the script at all. Surely, Samie supposed, the mentor was meant to express disappointment. And then she should issue a devastatingly strict set of guidelines to ensure the utmost integrity in the future. But instead, Margaret—this older, wiser, sage of a woman—was encouraging her to perpetrate the very misdemeanor she most desired to commit.

"So, why don't you just start dating?" Margaret repeated unhelpfully.

"B-but what about Siction Sex?" stammered Samie. "I mean Suction Six ..."

"Forget it!" interrupted Margaret with a girlish laugh and a dismissive wave of her hand. "The question is, what do you and Pete want?"

"But we made a commitment," retorted Samie, not used to being the sensible one in this—or any other—relationship. "We made a decision not to date, to set ourselves apart for God for the year ..."

"Well, it's up to you," smiled Margaret. "But let me know what you decide!"

And so we decided. We talked and realized that the heart behind Section Six was actually not bad. More importantly, we remembered that we had chosen to commit ourselves to singleness for a year for good reasons, regardless of any particular rule. Samie had recently split up from a serious relationship. Our team of six would be badly affected by a third of its members forming a rather exclusive sub-committee. And most of all, we both wanted to give God the best of our time for the rest of that year.

HEART TRANSPLANT

From that moment on, there was little doubt in our minds that, come the end of the year, we would begin dating without a moment's delay. But we decided that we would wait—not because of a rule, but simply out of a decision we had made in our own hearts. Even more than we wanted to defy Section Six, we found that we wanted to honor God.

83

I have absolutely no doubt that Margaret's wise advice to Samie that day helped lay the foundation for our marriage. Had she simply enforced the law, we would have found great delight in bending the rules or perhaps even breaking them, and this would have added a great deal of spice to each moment together! But by liberating us to choose for ourselves, Margaret unleashed the greatest power on earth—the power of grace. At that moment, the "should" of law became the "could" of grace. Where there had been a rigid rule, there was now a releasing gift that empowered us to "sin" if we wanted to, but also to be true—we could choose the best if we so desired, we could pay a price that seemed enormous, and yet would one day become something so much more.

The Bible talks precisely about the dynamics of Section Six versus the power of the heart-decision we made that day. It is the contrast between God's law and grace. Both law and grace are good—desiring the goal of healthy relationships. But where the Law of the Ten Commandments was written on cold tablets of stone as impersonal, insistent, and upright as Section Six ever was, grace—God's gift in the new covenant—is a different kind of law tattooed onto the walls of our beating hearts. "I will remove from you your heart of stone and give you a heart of flesh," God says through Ezekiel. "I will put my Spirit in you and move you to follow my decrees and be careful to keep my laws" (36:27).

Samie and I found ourselves mysteriously moved "to follow the decrees" of Section Six and strangely "careful to keep its laws" because Margaret had enabled us to make a heart decision. In the same way, when we become Christians, God's will is internalized so that we begin to want what Jesus wants.

With hindsight, it is obvious that the sacrifice Samie and I made to deny ourselves a few months of romance was in fact no sacrifice at all. It was a gateway to great joy. We had made a decision to "seek first his kingdom and his righteousness, and all these things" really had been given to us as well (Matthew 6:23).

The disciples of Jesus were often challenged to make sacrifices for Him, but the price they were asked to pay was consistently dwarfed by their desire to follow. To put it crudely, the sacrifices they made for Christ always seemed "worth it."

The way of discipleship—of covenant commitment and sacrificial worship—modeled by those first followers and explored in this book, is costly and hard. Anyone who says that it is easy to follow Jesus is a liar. He Himself said that the way is narrow. But nothing we forgo in the cause of Christ—wealth, popularity, kudos, not even our very lives—can come anywhere close to the return. The price we pay to follow Jesus—whatever it might be—will acquire for us the most astounding "bargain" of our lives![2]

"I tell you the truth," Jesus said to them, "no one who has left home or wife or

2. Dallas Willard describes the cost of discipleship as a "bargain" in his book, *The Divine Conspiracy*, chapter eight.

brothers or parents or children for the sake of the kingdom of God will fail to receive many times as much in this age and, in the age to come, eternal life."

When the Holy Spirit fills our lives, we begin to want what God wants and to see what God sees. In His grace, God interrupts our mundane little lives and calls us to follow. As we obey, our hearts are changed. The old covenant of our selfish motivation and "far-off" vision is replaced with a new covenant written on our hearts, and we now share God's priorities, longing for the fulfillment of His will whatever it may cost. The sacrifices of obedience are outweighed by the joy of being chosen to walk, one step at a time, in relationship with God.

86

CHAPTER EIGHT
WHEN GRACE GROWS UP

"Happy are they who know that discipleship simply means the life which springs from grace, and that grace simply means discipleship."
(Dietrich Bonhoeffer, The Cost of Discipleship)[1]

I was sitting in an upstairs living room in a multicultural area of Kansas City looking around at a circle of people—mostly in their twenties—listening as they shared honest stories about their spiritual struggles. A guy named Adam was speaking with candor. I knew him to be a gifted and diligent young leader, someone hungry for God, committed to study, soft-hearted, serious minded, and yet always up for a laugh. "I find myself responsible for a whole load of people," he was saying, his piercing blue eyes scanning the attentive circle, "and yet I feel like I'm failing them. The fact is," he continued quietly, his eyes now fixed with embarrassment on the floor at his feet, "The fact is, I hardly ever actually *pray* for all these people I'm leading." He paused and looked up: "What should I do?"

"Adam, don't beat yourself up!" someone piped up, a little too quickly.

"Yeah," chimed in another. "You're doing all you can—there are only so many hours in a day!"

Slowly, as if some invisible peace pipe was being passed round the circle, each member had his or her say. And they said such kind things:

"Go easy on yourself, Adam."

1. Dietrich Bonhoeffer, *The Cost of Discipleship* (SCM, London) p. 3.

"You're an incredible leader—don't get into condemnation."

"God loves you just the way you are."

"You can never pray enough anyway—don't fret."

An older man who looked like a biker shared a moving story about a time when God had actually told him to pray *less* in order to break out of the legalistic boxes of his daily devotional life.

As all these people spoke their lines, I studied Adam's face, and there, I saw a very interesting thing. All the kind words—well meant messages of grace and approval—seemed to be actually increasing the sadness in his eyes. For some reason, instead of bringing the joy they were intended to, these assurances appeared to be disappointing him even more.

"Maybe we're all missing something here," I said, thinking out loud. "I mean, everyone's speaking words of grace to you, Adam, but ..."

I paused, knowing what I wanted to say, but nervous that it might be misunderstood. "What if this isn't a guilt-trip?"

Adam was looking at me quizzically, but it was too late to turn back now. "What if this is the Holy Spirit speaking to you? Maybe God really is challenging you to pray more for the people you're leading, and you need to just get on and do it."

As I said this, a surprising thing happened: Adam's face lit up with relief. In part, he had, no doubt, wanted to hear the pampering of platitudes, but something else in him had indeed recognized the voice of the Holy Spirit and was therefore longing simply to obey!

Obedience is not legalism: Adam knows God will not love him more if he prays more. Neither is it masochism: Adam isn't trying to beat himself up in the name of Jesus. This is the most natural progression in the world—the heart of a son who is growing up and discovering that his Father "disciplines those He loves" and that such discipline, though "unpleasant at the time ... produces a harvest of righteousness and peace for those who have been trained by it" (Hebrews 12:6, 11).

ST. FRANCIS OF ASSISI

Many Christians revere Francis as one of the most Christ-like people who ever lived. The son of a wealthy Italian cloth merchant, he became a mercenary soldier and was taken prisoner in a violent skirmish with a neighboring city. After a year in jail, Francis became extremely ill and was released. During his convalescence back home, he began a spiritual journey. He was praying in the semi-derelict church of San Damiano one day when God spoke to him in an audible voice from the crucifix calling him simply to: "Rebuild my church." Those three words revolutionized Francis' life and the lives of many thousands to come. Right away, he renounced all his (considerable) worldly wealth and thus began an astonishing life begging from the rich, giving to the poor, preaching the Gospel, and attracting many followers through his kindness, humility, and joyful sacrifice.

The greatest heroes of our faith have always been those like St. Francis of Assisi, Florence Nightingale, and Martin Luther King Jr., who responded to God's love with extraordinary personal sacrifice. But as I look around the Church at this time, I see a real danger looming: I am concerned that the message of grace, which is currently being propounded so passionately from pulpits and paperbacks around the world, might merely become a "license to chill"—an all-embracing, one-size-fits-all, mindless rationale for accepting the greatest comfort and personal pleasure in any given situation. Such an aberration of grace labels those who break its code—those people like Adam who are seeking to be more disciplined and sacrificial in their faith—"religious," "pious," "driven," "culturally irrelevant," "caught up in good works," "perfectionistic," or simply "legalistsic."

89

THE "ME" MANTRA

Of course, there is an ever-present danger of legalism and unhealthy pietism in the Church at large, and we all need to be told to relax at times, to be reminded and re-assured of God's love and endless mercy. But in a culture forsworn to self-gratification, the danger far greater to us than legalism is surely the tendency toward the deification of pleasure in the name of grace.

- The spirit of the age says, "Learn to love yourself," and I've heard plenty of sermons by well-meaning pastors that echoed this refrain. But Jesus says the exact opposite: "The man who loves his life will lose it, while the man who hates his life in this world will keep it for eternal life" (John 12:25).
- The spirit of the age says, "Look after number one." But Jesus says, "If anyone wants to be first, he must be the very last, and the servant of all" (Mark 9:35). It's a model of leadership that is preached often, but seldom practiced in business, in government, and even in church.
- The spirit of the age says, "Go easy on yourself." But Paul says: "No, I beat my body and make it my slave so that after I have preached to others, I myself will not be disqualified for the prize" (1 Corinthians 9:27).

Grace is calling us to "give up the game of minimum integrity." Too often we are reduced to trivial debates about how far we can go sexually or how much we should give financially—all the shades of gray in the ethics of obedience. And I suppose if we are mere adherents to a religious code, then such negotiations are fine and necessary. But if we are caught up in an infatuation of the holy, if this is a religion of living relationship and burning passion, then the impulse will not be to get the best deal, but rather, to give with joyful extravagance. When in doubt, we will not try to negotiate the minimum personal outlay, but rather, will go the extra mile (Matthew 5:39-42).

MILK TEETH

The message of grace has come right to the forefront over recent years. Some of the most gifted spiritual teachers of our age have devoted the best part of their lives to proclaiming the unconditional kindness of God. Let me say very clearly that I consider their message of grace to be directly from God's heart, and we must never stop proclaiming and celebrating the fact that grace is the essence of the Gospel and the foundation of our faith. But in our generation, I believe the Holy Spirit is bringing a new word to the forefront to fill conversations and aspirations the way grace has for the last ten to twenty years. It is a word used more than twice as often as "grace" in the New Testament, and yet it is taught far less in the contemporary Church. The word is: "discipleship."

It's not that the era of grace is over and that we are now moving into an era of harsh discipline (perish the thought), but rather that *grace must grow up!* At first, like a baby, we are fed, cuddled, and cared for by unconditional parental love. This love remains unconditional throughout our lives, but as we grow in its care, we learn to feed ourselves, to dress ourselves, to discipline and direct our own lives. And then we leave home to become parents ourselves, no longer simply receiving grace, but dispensing it to our own children, often at great personal cost. The grace in which we were nurtured has thus grown to maturity.

91

"Anyone who lives on milk, being still an infant, is not acquainted with the teaching about righteousness. But solid food is for the mature, who by constant use have trained themselves to distinguish good from evil. Therefore let us leave the elementary teachings about Christ and go on to maturity" (Hebrews 5:13-6:1).

BONHOEFFER

Dietrich Bonhoeffer was a brave and brilliant German pastor during the second World War who became a double agent in an attempt to bring down Hitler and in 1943, was imprisoned without trial for his part in smuggling fourteen Jews to Switzerland. At the start of the war, he turned down the offer of a safe job in America, convinced that his Christian duty was to stay and face the evils of Hitler.

As a young man, Bonhoeffer must have been sorely tempted to swap the terror of war for a safe passage to a leafy American seminary. However, such temptations to compromise are famously attributed by Bonhoeffer to a theology of "cheap grace ... the deadly enemy of our Church," adding, "We are fighting today for costly grace."[2] Bonhoeffer fought that battle for costly grace in Nazi Germany, seeking to gather a Church that would dare to be different from the cultural norms of Hitler's social program. As a result, he was executed at the age of thirty-nine, just days before the end of the war, having lived the life and died the death of costly discipleship. "Christianity without discipleship," he wrote, "is always Christianity without Christ. It remains an abstract idea, a myth which has a place for the Fatherhood of God, but omits Christ as the living Son. ... There is trust in God, but no following of Christ."[3] Fatherhood without following. Christianity without discipleship. Bonhoeffer's words are as disturbing and relevant today as they were in Nazi Germany.

CYANIDE PILL

> *"Anyone, who does not carry his cross and follow me, cannot be my disciple." (Luke 14:27)*

A pastor was once showing the theologian Clarence Jordan around his church. No expense had been spared. Pointing at the neon cross glowing on top of the steeple, the pastor boasted, "That cross alone cost us $10,000." Clarence looked at him and said, "You got cheated. Times were when Christians could get them for free."

Bonhoeffer's fight for costly grace is, I fear, to be the fight of our generation, too. We are spending more money on ministry than ever before, yet our

2. Ibid.
3. Ibid., 64.

churches are in decline. "Worship" alone is a multi-million dollar industry with its own celebrities—there is even an annual award ceremony to honor the most "successful" worship leaders. Meanwhile, Christian books top the New York Best Seller List; we have conferences, programs, training courses, kids' camps, and a myriad of ministries, models, and sure-fire methods ... the catalog is endless. And these things are not bad. In fact, some of these things are very good. But I sometimes imagine a Middle Eastern carpenter stepping into this spiritual frenzy (every last stitch and syllable conducted in His name), and as He looks around, smiling sadly at the crowds—all that aching desperation gathered in some vast exhibition center—He issues a simple invitation:

"Anyone," He begins, His voice echoing slightly around the auditorium, "who does not carry his cross and follow me, cannot be my disciple" (Luke 14:27). And with that, He turns His back on the booths, the huddles, the multicolored banners saying, "*Smile, Jesus Loves You!*" and disappears through the narrow door at the back of the building. And I wonder how many will follow. I wonder if I will follow.

93

As members of such a selfish generation, we must remind ourselves continually that the way—the only way—to apprentice ourselves to Jesus is to sacrifice our rights, allow the lethal injection, take the cyanide pill in whatever guise it comes, and follow.

But why should we?

One morning, not long after He had risen from the dead, Jesus sat on a stony beach by Galilee cooking for His friends. The smell of the smoke rose in the still morning air, the fish meat hissed, and Jesus sat by the fire waiting for a moment to talk to Peter alone. The conversation came (it was painful), and it went. And having re-commissioned His friend, Jesus warned him of the fate he would face should he continue to follow: "When you are old you will stretch out your hands, and someone else will dress you and lead you where you do not want to go." John clarifies that: "Jesus said this to indicate the kind of death by which Peter would glorify God." And on this devastating note, Jesus "turned to him and said, 'Follow me!'" (John 21:18-19).

Peter obeyed, following faithfully for the rest of his life. He fathered the Church, he pioneered her mission to the Gentiles, and then, as an old man, legend has it that he was forced to watch his wife be crucified in the authorities' attempt to make "The Rock" recant. When he would not deny his Lord a fourth time, they crucified him, too—upside-down at his own request because he maintained that he was not worthy to share the death of his Master.

Why did he do it? Why, on that beach that day when he received the big tip off, did he not just say a polite "thanks but no thanks"?

Because for Peter, there was no other life worth living and no other death worth dying. Obedience, for him, was not a personal lifestyle choice; it was an eternal call from God Himself, spoken directly through Christ, Peter's Friend, Savior, and Lord. Who was he to refuse?

94

Church history is full of those, like Peter, who paid the ultimate price in following Jesus. Polycarp served faithfully as bishop of Smyrna (Izmir in modern day Turkey) at the beginning of the second century. Eventually he was arrested, and the Roman proconsul took pity on such a gentle old man, urging him to proclaim, "Caesar is Lord." If Polycarp would make this declaration and offer a small pinch of incense to Caesar's statue, he would escape torture and death. But in response, Polycarp made his celebrated reply: "Fourscore and six years have I served Him, and he has done me no harm. How then can I curse my King that saved me?" Steadfast in his commitment to Christ, Polycarp refused to compromise his beliefs, and thus, was burned alive at the stake. Few of us will face such a trial, but we are all called to die daily to our own desires and to live in obedience to Christ.

And so Jesus comes to us and invites us to follow whatever the cost. He promises us hardship, persecution, and pain. And then He says, "Follow me!"

THE DOG THAT DIED

"The great tragedy of modern evangelism," wrote Jim Wallis, "is in calling many people to belief but few to obedience."[4] And the great tragedy of that lament is that it was made thirty years ago, and nothing much has changed. In fact, for want of a radical challenge, the Church seems to be drowning herself in a sea of shallow grace. One recent survey says that 85 percent of American men do not feel "spiritually challenged," while on the other side of the Atlantic, one in twelve British women are using anti-depressants.[5] The number of unchurched Americans, according to the Barna Research Group, has almost doubled since 1991, and sadly, the statistics in Europe are worse.[6] This is not a game—it really is judgment day for the "House of the Lord": If the message of grace we are currently preaching, teaching, and making so much of really is true grace—the costly kind—it will grow up in us and produce mature disciples willing to do whatever it takes to love and live for God.

95

Throughout history, whenever God's people have lost their way, He has intervened by sending messengers to call us back to obedience: people like Polycarp, Francis, and Bonhoeffer who cry out prophetically in the wilderness. As G.K. Chesterton wrote a hundred years ago, "At least five times ... the Faith has to all appearance gone to the dogs. In each of these five cases it was the dog that died."[7] Amidst the nominalism of consumer-Christianity, there is an increasing number of people in whom the message of grace is bearing fruit. These people, wherever I meet them, are longing—even craving—to move on from the milk of elementary teachings about grace to the meat of mature discipleship. They are signs of great hope that God is commissioning a Gideon's army in our time, nurturing a "root of Jesse" once again.[8]

4. Jim Wallis, *Agenda for Biblical People* (HarperCollins, New York, NY: 1976) p. 23.
5. Barna Research Group survey for Promise Keepers, released April 28, 2004, and British Government Report, published September 1998.
6. Barna Research Group survey 1991-2004, released May 5, 2004.
7. G.K. Chesterton, *The Everlasting Man* (Ignatius, San Francisco, CA: 1993) p. 274.
8. Isaiah 11:1—The Old Testament theme of a godly remnant out of which new life shall spring, ultimately fulfilled in Christ.

CHAPTER NINE
WHEN JESUS SAYS "GO"

$\mathcal{M}$onty Python's *Monty Python and the Search for the Holy Grail* depicts a hilarious confrontation between King Arthur and the Black Knight who is guarding a bridge.

"I command you, as King of the Britons, to stand aside!" bellows Arthur.

"I move for no man!" replies the Knight.

"So be it," says Arthur, deftly chopping off the Black Knight's left arm. "Now stand aside, worthy adversary."

"'Tis but a scratch."

"A scratch? Your arm's off!"

The Black Knight flatly refuses to acknowledge the amputation, and another sword fight ensues. This time, Arthur removes the unfortunate Knight's other arm: "Victory is mine!" he declares, kneeling to thank God, until his prayer is interrupted by a defiant cry from the Black Knight.

"Oh, had enough, eh?"

"Look," yells Arthur in exasperation. "You've got no arms left!"

"'Tis just a flesh wound!" exclaims the Black Knight, kicking the king, who retaliates by lopping one of his legs off.

"Right. I'll do you for that!" cries the Knight undeterred, hopping around on his one remaining limb. "I'm invincible! The Black Knight always triumphs!"

When he loses his other leg, the Knight (now limbless) grudgingly offers to concede a draw. Finally, Arthur rides off under a hail of protest:

"Oh, I see. Running away, eh? Come back here and take what's coming to you. I'll bite your legs off!"

I sometimes think the Church in the West is like the Black Knight, hopping around yelling, "I'm invincible!" and challenging the devil to the most improbable of fights. We continue to issue our war cries and defiant ultimatums to anyone who will listen, when in fact, we are a wounded body, unable at this time to stand and fight the way we should.

It's perfectly true that we are "invincible." Jesus promises: "I will build my church, and the gates of Hades will not overcome it" (Matthew 16:18). But the wounds we have suffered are real and deep. If the body of Christ is to stand, fight, and walk effectively in our generation, it will be upon the two legs of intimacy and involvement.

INTIMACY AND INVOLVEMENT

The devil is determined to prevent the Church from rising up and walking. He will do anything to cripple our intimacy with God or our involvement in society—or both. Without the leg of active involvement, we hop around on the spot in an intimate spiritual ghetto with few non-Christian friends and little social impact, requiring programs and projects just to help us make meaningful contact with the wider world. We are inspired but irrelevant. On the other hand (or rather, leg), involvement without intimacy leaves us spiritually ineffective, dangerously vulnerable to misunderstanding and compromise. Prayer becomes a rubber stamp for our own plans, rather than a rudder to steer our thoughts and actions. We end up stressing out with Martha in the kitchen, while Mary sits at Jesus' feet, having "chosen what is better" (Luke 10:42).

"The Vision" describes this balance as the call to "pray like it all depends upon God" while living "like it all depends on us."[1] Whenever the body of Christ

---

1. No one really knows who originated this phrase. It has been attributed to everyone from St. Augustine and St. Francis of Assisi to General William Booth and Moody!

combines intimacy with involvement, she walks the corridors of power, she dances with the meek, she stands up for the rights of the poor, and she does all this with a true heart of worship both offensive and attractive to a watching world.

We need to strike this balance between intimacy and involvement at every level of discipleship.

- Personally—in our own private walks with God.
- Congregationally—in our local church communities.
- Generationally—in the army God is commissioning.

1. INTIMACY AND INVOLVEMENT: MY PERSONAL WALK

Physically, I am right-handed, and spiritually, I have a preferred side, too—a bias toward involvement rather than intimacy. As a result, the Holy Spirit often has to call me to exodus into God's presence (while rarely needing to remind me to engage). I'm learning—slowly—to recognize His whispered invitations to withdraw, to defy a little logic by waiting a while, to deny the demands of my schedule and sit listening at His feet with Mary. I'm not good at this waiting game, but I'm learning. For other people, the pull is the other way—their natural tendency is more contemplative, less pragmatic, and they require regular reminders to "go," to "move," to sacrifice comfort and risk a little failure, too.

99

In order to maintain the pace of our spiritual journey through the seasons of time, it is essential to develop our own personal disciplines—rhythms and even Rules of Life (see chapter 13)—which help us balance intimacy and involvement by listening regularly for the redress of the Spirit in the Word of God.

> *"Whether you turn to the right or to the left, your ears will hear a voice behind you, saying, 'This is the way; walk in it.'"*
> *(Isaiah 30:21)*

2. INTIMACY AND INVOLVEMENT: THE CONGREGATION ON THE MOVE

In order to build communities that are both intimate and involved, Christians must learn to appreciate those brothers and sisters whose instincts contrast their own. Mature church leaders learn to rejoice in the creative tension between activists and contemplatives, intercessors and evangelists, artists and entrepreneurs, introverts and extroverts, the well-worn ruts of the older Christians and the off-road extremes of the new believers. Secure leadership will not try to ameliorate either extreme, because these differences are God's way of ensuring that both legs of the body are working together. Properly handled, the paradoxes of community can create movement and life.

3. INTIMACY AND INVOLVEMENT: A GENERATION WITH ITS MARCHING ORDERS

Every generation must take its place in history, asking what it means to be a truly prophetic community in their own era. Sometimes God calls a group of His people to exodus—to flee the slavery of Egypt, cross the Red Sea, and wander in the wilderness as an exclusive, nomadic clan. But at other times, God calls His people to do the opposite—to cross the Jordan River in order to possess and populate the Promised Land.

For the people of Israel, both crossings were miraculous. Both required godly leadership. Both were Spirit-led movements for the times in which they were living. The issue was—and is always—one of sensitivity and obedience to the immediate guidance of God.

In the previous chapter, I made my conviction clear: I believe the Holy Spirit is calling us at this time to grow up in grace and to move from a message of inward-looking intimacy with the Father to active and sacrificial engagement with the pain and the sin of the world. It's time to get our boots muddy—to cross the Jordan and inhabit the land. Having invited us to "come," Jesus is now commanding us to "go" and make disciples in every nation.

If I am right, then there is a cultural shift coming to the Church in every area. Take, for instance, our understanding of worship. Over the last twenty years, we have experienced a glorious renewal in worship (by which we tend to mean the musical aspects of congregational life). But now it is time for an equally glorious renewal in the other great dimension of worship: justice for the poor.

DAILY BREAD

"The Vision" describes a generation of disciples who are "free yet they are slaves of the hurting and dirty and dying." But sometimes, surrounded by unspeakable pain and sin, it's easy to feel helpless. A few months ago, I failed completely. I was in Macedonia, a war-torn Balkan nation with 50 percent unemployment and no state security. Old ladies scrabble through garbage beside the roads. Boys sell drugs. Girls sell their bodies.

Lunchtime found me sitting in an open-air restaurant on a pleasant spring day eating a delicious Greek salad. A stream of street-sellers and beggars were coming to the tables in the hope of a coin or two.

101

I finished my meal, leaving a large loaf of warm bread uneaten. I'd been chatting to a Scottish lady at the next table who turned out to be in Macedonia on business, and she knew by now that I was a Christian. "How should we respond to all these beggars?" she asked. "I feel so guilty!"

Just then, a woman wearing a black headscarf approached me with her hands outstretched for a crust or a coin. I'd been advised to ignore such demands—there are many good reasons for doing so. And so, I gave the Scottish woman my informed opinion about the importance of listening to one's conscience and actively addressing the root causes of poverty, while giving nothing to the beggar.

That night, I was troubled and found myself re-playing the conversation in my head, sensing that something had been wrong. And then it hit me: I had blanked Jesus out while trying to talk about Him. How desperately that little lady must have craved the warm loaf of bread, discarded by my plate. How easily I could have offered her the dignity of a seat at my table and a piece of my meal, but I realized with remorse that I couldn't even recall her face. How much more like my Lord it would have been to have broken the rules, by-passed a little common-sense, and looked deep into those eyes for a name and a story. Instead, I had offered a pompous sermon about the root causes of poverty. What a hypocrite I am. What a beggar. I asked Jesus to forgive me, "for," as He said, "I was hungry and you gave me nothing to eat" (Matthew 25:42).

Jesus summarized His mission on earth like this:

> *"The Spirit of the Lord is on me,*
> *because he has anointed me to preach good news to the poor.*
> *He has sent me to proclaim freedom for the prisoner*
> *and recovery of sight for the blind,*
> *to release the oppressed, to proclaim the year of the Lord's favor."*
> *(Luke 4:18-19)*

The Spirit of God anoints us to worship with singing, but also by engaging with the pain of the real world. He has commissioned us to involve ourselves, actively and compassionately, with the neediest members of society. The stinging rebuke spoken through Amos (6:21-24) surely challenges our generation, too, to incorporate Christ's mission to the poor as an integral expression of our worship. My fear is that, unless we begin to pour our passion for music and meetings into the poor and needy as well, the wonderful harmonies of our praise may soon become distorted in the ears of God.

> *"If you do away with the yoke of oppression,*
> *with the pointing finger and malicious talk,*

and if you spend yourselves on behalf of the hungry
and satisfy the needs of the oppressed,
then your light will rise in the darkness,
and your night will become like the noonday."
(Isaiah 58:9-10)

Let's not stop writing and singing extravagant songs of worship. Let's continue to rejoice with all our hearts—there are times to pour expensive perfume on the feet of Christ, knowing that the poor will always be with us (Matthew 26:11). But there are also times to turn over the tables of corruption in the temple, outraged that the poor are being neglected and abused in the very courts of worship (Matthew 21:13).

What does all this mean in reality? For each one of us, the challenge is very practical:

- It means a radical review of our giving and what we do with our money.
- It means that we wear less designer label clothing because we have seen through the underlying value system.
- It means choosing a less impressive company car because it will guzzle less gas.
- It means that every single Christian is called to cultivate a genuine friendship with someone society marginalizes.
- It means taking time to talk with the lonely widower at the end of the meeting when our friends are leaving without us.
- Isaiah says that it means employers not driving their staffs so hard (58:3); it means "inviting the homeless poor into your homes," "being available to your own families" (58:7 MSG), and putting

away "the pointing finger and malicious talk" (58:9).

As churches, the call to justice may mean:

- One less worship pastor and one more ministry to the marginalized. I long for the time when the job description of every professional worship leader will involve working at least one day a week among the poor and finding the face of Christ there (Matthew 25:40).
- The call to justice might also involve an audit of our teaching so that the pulpit begins to nurture a spirituality that is earthier and more immediate, expounding on the scriptures that help us become more socially and politically literate. As Bonhoeffer used to say: "It is not only my task to look after the victims of madmen who drive a motorcar down a crowded street, but to do all in my power to stop their driving at all."

RESIDENT ALIENS

Of course, the challenge to "go" into all the earth and involve ourselves in society should not eclipse our distinctive identity in Christ or lead us to love the culture indiscriminately. Although Peter urges us to live "as aliens and strangers in the world" (1 Peter 2:11) and Jesus said the world would hate and persecute us (John 15), I confess that I often find myself remarkably comfortable here. In seeking to involve ourselves in the culture, there is an ever-present danger of "assimilation"—becoming indistinguishable from the world in which we are living. *GQ* magazine wrote a feature about Evangelical Christians, which concluded woefully that we are essentially a Xerox copy of the wider culture—not markedly different in any way.

Samie and I once led a team planting a student congregation in the city of Portsmouth, U.K., that was granted permission to meet once a month in the university nightclub. Excitedly, the team began planning the first meeting: the music we would play, the content, the simple rituals and potent visuals. We decided on everything very quickly—except for one important aspect of the event: the name. It needed to sound cool and non-religious enough to attract non-churchgoers, but, after devoting way too much time to discussing the branding of the event, someone spoke up in exasperation: "Who cares what the stupid name is? Let's just call it what it is!"

And so we did. Our super-cool church service in the student club was christened without any imagination at all—simply "church," because that was exactly what it was. And the funny thing about this name was that non-churchgoers were fascinated.

"Cool name. What is it?"

"Um—it's church."

"Yeah, but what is it?"

"That's what it actually is ..."

"Church?"

"Yep!"

"As in, like, God and stuff?"

"Hopefully."

"In the bar?"

"Where else?"

"Wow!"

"Wanna come?"

"To church?"

"Yes."

Sometimes it is when we stop trying to be relevant that we actually become relevant to a watching world. Our "irrelevance" may well be the very message the world is looking for at this time. Sometimes we will be called to defy the culture—never to deify it—by living biblically and modeling a different way of being a student, a musician, a teacher, or whatever world we have been sent to inhabit.

In his book *Prophetic Untimeliness*, Os Guinness rues the fact that, "never have Christians pursued relevance more strenuously" than we currently do, and yet "never have Christians been more irrelevant."[2] He attributes this sad state of affairs to a number of factors, not least that "a great part of the evangelical community has transferred authority from *Sola Scriptura* to *Sola Cultura*."[3] In other words, we are being shaped more by the culture around us than we are by the Bible.

We must beware all the talk among trendy Christians of cultural relevance. During its first three hundred years, the Church grew exponentially, and yet it was radically committed to a biblical lifestyle that often clashed with the prevailing culture: "every Christian by definition was a candidate for death. To understate: if one wanted a soft life, or to get ahead in respectable circles, one did not become a Christian."[4]

106

These Christians were in the world but resiliently not of it. Their power lay in their purity. Their cultural relevance was rooted not in such superficialities as the clothes they wore or the music they listened to, but rather in their spectacular divergence from the cultural norm. *GQ* magazine would certainly have been startled by this subversive, alternative network of underground communities nurturing a fundamentally different worldview and multiplying in spite of persecution throughout the earth. The word they adopted from the culture to describe themselves was the socio-legal term *paroikoi*—resident aliens.[5] They knew that they didn't belong.

In the Sermon on the Mount, Jesus uses two contrasting metaphors to describe our Christian witness. He says that we are to be like salt that seasons society, and yet also like a city on a hill, visible but distinct. The Early Church was both salt

2. Os Guinness, *Prophetic Untimeliness* (Baker Books: 2003) p. 12.
3. Ibid. p. 45
4. Alan Kreider, *Worship and Evangelism in Pre-Christendom* (Grove Books, Cambridge: 1995) p. 6.
5. See also Ephesians 2:1; 1 Peter 2:11.

in society and a distinct city on a hill, culturally present, but different, and thus, in their difference, they were relevant, attracting converts and persecution alike. Such could be the signs of our times—the fruit of a community worshiping Jesus in Spirit and in truth, marrying precious intimacy with practical involvement.

They huffed and puffed their way up the mountain overlooking the sparkling Sea of Galilee, the fitter disciples pausing occasionally to allow the others to catch up.

"Why couldn't Jesus have told us to meet Him on the beach?" grumbled Thomas.

"Or in a boat," said James, eyeing a shoal of fish darkening the water below.

"Nothing wrong with the city," Matthew said, mopping sweat from his brow.

But the banter belied their excitement. All day there had been an unspoken consensus that this was about to be "it," and there were at least eleven different theories about what "it" might be.

Reaching the top of the hill, they sat gazing down at familiar landmarks, shadows of clouds the size of empires meandering across the sea, and even Matthew conceded that Galilee could be beautiful on a day like this. But such conversation soon dissipated as each of the eleven disciples waited and watched, lost in his own thoughts.

It was John who saw Him first—he always seemed to know where to look—and let out a single cry of recognition. An unusual stillness seemed to envelop the whole mountain as the disciples instinctively stood, gathered around the Lord, and sank to their knees without a single word exchanged. Even Peter knew this was no time for talking. Jesus made no attempt to sit, but stood in the middle of the group, gazing down at each face in turn, silently exploring the familiar features with evident affection.

The next day, they would reflect and agree: Jesus had seemed excited. It had reminded them of the eager anticipation in His eyes on the day He first said "come" to each one of them. He had seemed excited like the time they had returned to His side with reports of demons obeying and sicknesses cured. Excited like the day He rode the donkey into Jerusalem as the crowds cried out "Hosanna!" Excited to be returning to His Father, at last, His mission accomplished.

"And the power," said Matthew. "Did you feel it?" They all nodded. They had felt such things before; when a centurion or a member of the Sanhedrin came near, you could sometimes feel a certain energy emanating from their presence. But the power from Jesus that day was stronger and infinitely more beautiful, like an invisible light blinding you, or a silent rumble of thunder, and the closer He came, the brighter and louder it seemed.

108

On the mountain, Jesus was studying each of the men in turn. Peter's face had aged much more than three years, but it was still as open and strong as the first time they had met. In John's brown eyes, the tears were welling up, and his chest was heaving—he had always been the first to worship and probably always would be. Thomas' expression was more complicated, less certain, struggling to believe his own eyes, his mind flailing frantically for some explanation—any other explanation—to the impossible truth before him now. Jesus smiled softly and winked so quickly that Thomas blinked and wondered if he had seen it at all. Several others, like Thomas, doubted their eyes, yet none failed to worship that day.

No one had noticed the cloud shadow—and perhaps it was coincidence—but as Jesus raised His hands to speak, the sun came out.

"All authority," He said, "in heaven and on earth has been given to me."

They knew it was true: They could *feel* it—the silent thunder of His presence—

and they had seen it.

"Therefore," He paused. Everything paused. The excitement was palpable. This, they knew, was "it" ...

"Go and make disciples of all nations, baptizing them in the name of the Father and of the Son and of the Holy Spirit, and teaching them to obey everything I have commanded you."

Jesus of Nazareth took one last look around the little group of men with whom He had shared everything for three years. Each one was absorbing every word, every syllable and nuance. Each one was feeling loved as if the others were not there.

"And surely I am," He paused again and smiled, allowing the last two words to resonate, "I *am* with you always, to the very end of the age."

And with that, Jesus returned to the Father. The wind began to blow once more, and the eleven disciples became aware again of the presence of the others. It seemed an eternity ago that Jesus of Nazareth had invited each one of them to "come." Without a care in the world, they had followed, and it had been more wonderful and more terrible than they could ever have foreseen. And now this same Jesus—the very Son of God—who had called them to come, had commissioned them to "Go ..."

They took their first few steps in silence, hardly daring to speak, and as they trudged down the mountain, the world seemed to shrink under their feet. Galilee, Jerusalem, Judea, and distant lands undiscovered by Caesar himself would no longer—could no longer—contain this Gospel of the kingdom, this divine assignment suddenly ignited in their hearts. It was the message of the covenant, the promise of God to Abraham, Moses, and David that "all nations on earth will be blessed, because you have obeyed me" (Genesis 22:17-18).

The disciples walked down the hill, carrying this great commission, and they simply never stopped moving until the day they died. Like lava flowing from an erupting volcano, they just kept going from the top of that mountain to the ends of the earth—"resident aliens" wherever they went, proclaiming the story, the glory of a carpenter from Nazareth, who is Christ of all cultures, High King of heaven, Savior, Friend, and Lord.

He chose us, too, to come to His side and commissioned us, like them, to go to the nations. One day soon, Jesus will call us to come to His side again, and on that day, there will be no more going—grace will be complete. We will be home at last with Him, forever.

"I will establish my covenant as an everlasting covenant between me and you and your descendants after you for the generations to come, to be your God and the God of your descendants after you ..."
(Deuteronomy 17:7)

"Their DNA chooses Jesus,
He breathes out, they breathe in,
their subconscious sings,
they had a blood transfusion with Jesus."

the VISION and

the VOW

COVENANT

SACRIFICE FUELS THE FIRE...

CHAPTER TEN
PROMISE

"And foreigners who bind themselves to the Lord ...
who hold fast to my covenant—
these I will bring to my holy mountain
and give them joy in my house of prayer."
(Isaiah 56:6-7)

In the movie *Four Weddings and a Funeral*, Hugh Grant's character finds himself at the altar about to make his vows, for all the wrong reasons, to a woman he doesn't really like, let alone love. The scene is set like any other wedding—the congregation in their suits and hats, the rings and the rites awaiting the bride and groom—but instead of heaven, this is hell. He is about to enter into a loveless covenant. His imminent commitment threatens slavery and dread instead of joy and liberty. Why? Because the words exchanged in the ceremony of marriage matter; they are far more than mere resolutions, they are vows—not easily undone. A couple in love long to make such promises; they buy rings in their desire to be bound by law to one another for life. But without love, the very same prospect becomes perverse, the promise a prison, and the dream a nightmare.

This section of the book—entitled "Covenant"—has three chapters:

- Promise
- Conspiracy
- Order

Such words will sound formidable to some, but fascinating to others for whom grace is growing up—those looking to go deeper in their relationships with God. For them, this section could be the exhilarating next step on their personal path of discipleship, as exciting to them as the covenant of marriage for a couple in love. If you have reached such a point in your pilgrimage, these chapters may well excite your heart more than any others. But if you find yourself turned off by the challenges ahead, please just ignore them. Perhaps this is not yet your time for such vows, or perhaps you already have a disciplined and focused life. Either way, I encourage you simply to enjoy the stage of the journey in which you are.

WORD GAMES

We live in a culture that no longer truly understands the concept of covenant, nor the power of a vow. Couples take out pre-nuptial agreements as a get-out clause for the promise they are about to make. Business deals require an army of attorneys because the shaking of hands between "gentlemen" no longer means very much. Fewer medical students each year see any point in swearing the twenty-three-hundred-year-old Hippocratic Oath, promising to protect human life and treat patients with dignity.

As disciples of Jesus, we are called to be careful in the commitments we allow ourselves to make: "Simply let your 'Yes' be 'Yes,' and your 'No,' 'No,'" Jesus advised, "anything beyond this comes from the evil one" (Matthew 5:37).

Jesus is not forbidding the making of vows here—both the Old and New Testaments are full of such covenants. Rather, He is calling us to apply caution and integrity in all we say.

WORD POWER

Gradually, our culture is becoming less faithful and more stressful, suspicious, and cynical as words crumble and trust erodes from the schoolyard to the Senate and from Parliament to the press.

A school conducted an interesting experiment to ascertain the power of affirmation. They held a mock IQ test and broadcast the results, pointing out the "outstanding" students expected to do especially well in the coming year. Although the named children were really no brighter than anyone else, every one of them improved significantly in their academic performance over the course of the year. By being told that they were better, they had begun to believe they were better, and by believing they were better, they had actually *become* better. This is the extraordinary power of the spoken word to shape faith and the power of faith to alter reality.

If an impersonal blessing from a school teacher can have such significant impact, we can only imagine the power of more intimate and targeted words to build up or destroy. No wonder Jesus commands us to break the downward spiral of cheap speech and simply let our yes mean yes and our no mean no.

The book of James uses a succession of pictures to emphasize this power of the human tongue: "A word out of your mouth may seem of no account, but it can accomplish nearly anything—or destroy it! It only takes a spark, remember, to set off a forest fire. A careless or wrongly placed word out of your mouth can do that" (James 3:5 MSG).

The words we speak—and especially the promises we make—matter. In fact, as Paul emphasises to the Church in Rome, our words are as important as our beliefs in the process of our salvation:

"'The word is near you; it is in your mouth and in your heart,' that is, the word of faith we are proclaiming: That if you confess with your mouth, 'Jesus is Lord,' and believe in your heart that God raised him from the dead, you will be saved. For it is with your heart that you believe and are justified, and it is with your mouth that you confess and are saved" (Romans 10:8-9).

Words are also vital in the salvation of others, for, as Paul continues:

"'Everyone who calls on the name of the Lord will be saved.' How, then, can they call on the one they have not believed in? And how can they believe in the one of whom they have not heard? And how can they hear without someone preaching to them?" (10: 13-14).

CHILDREN OF PROMISE

It is not our words in and of themselves that bring salvation, but rather our words in response to God's Word—His covenant promise to us through which we are blessed. The concept of covenant is one of the keys to understanding the entire Bible story—the book we call the Word of God. Yahweh promised to bless the children of Abraham forever. This means that if, through faith in Jesus, we have become children of Abraham (Galations 3:14-29), we can be sure that God will bless us and make us fruitful, not because we deserve it, but because of His eternal promise to Abraham. As Christians, we are therefore directly affected on a daily basis by the Abrahamic covenant:

118

> *"I swear by myself, declares the Lord ... I will surely bless you and make*
> *your descendants as numerous as the stars in the sky and as the sand*
> *on the seashore. Your descendants will take possession of the cities of*
> *their enemies, and through your offspring all nations on earth will be*
> *blessed, because you have obeyed me."*
> *(Genesis 22:13-15)*

This promise to Abraham was reiterated to Moses and then extended to David as a Messianic hope of a Son who would one day reign eternally. This is why Jesus is introduced in the first verse of the New Testament as "Son of Abraham, Son of David." "Here he is," Matthew says, "the One who fulfils the two great covenants between God and man!" And having fulfilled these promises, Jesus established a "new covenant in [His] blood" by dying on the cross (Luke 22:20). This new covenant, written on our hearts, has—as we have already seen—the unique power to rewire our motivation toward good and God and away from death and destruction.

CUTTING A COVENANT

The Hebrew verb that describes the act of making a covenant literally means "to cut a covenant." This is a reference to the gory, ancient practice of cutting an animal carcass in half down the spine when a covenant was forged between two parties. The halves of the slaughtered sheep, donkey, or bull were then laid side by side on the ground, and the parties would declare their promises to one another before walking through the blood between the two parts. This act of walking through the blood was seen as the moment when the covenant became binding.

Having exchanged vows and walked between the broken body, one half would be ignited as a burnt offering to God, while the other would be cooked and eaten in a joyful feast of fellowship, celebrating the new relationship just begun.

119

This ritual has fascinating parallels with Jesus' "new covenant." At the Passover Feast—the Last Supper—He symbolically broke the bread in half saying: "This is my body given for you; do this in remembrance of me." The disciples almost certainly understood the covenant-cutting imagery as Jesus divided the loaf in this way. Next Jesus took the cup, and made the imagery explicit: "This cup is the new covenant in my blood, which is poured out for you." Every time we participate in the symbolic feast of communion, we are remembering that our relationship with God is a covenant, cut in His own Son's corpse. As we drink the wine, we walk through the blood of His broken body into a new relationship with God. In this covenant feast, God's promises are activated in our lives through the obedience of Jesus Christ, "Son of Abraham, Son of David," and we respond to the blessings of the covenant with our own grateful pledge of allegiance.

☨HE NAZIRITE VOW

Scripture recounts covenants with God and covenants between people, but it also talks about internal covenants we make with ourselves.

For example, Job tells us: "I made a covenant with my eyes not to look lustfully at a girl" (31:1), and the Apostle Paul "had his hair cut off at Cenchrea because of a vow he had taken" (Acts 18:18). This was almost certainly a Nazirite vow, similar to that undertaken by Samson and John the Baptist, and described in the book of Numbers as: "a vow of separation to the Lord" (6:2).

A Nazirite vow was an act of consecration, undertaken by a man or a woman for a limited period of time. This inward separation was outwardly expressed in abstinence from:

1. alcohol (and any fruit of the vine)
2. contact with corpses
3. haircuts.

At the completion of such a season of consecration, the Nazirite would ritually shave his head and burn his "dedicated" hair as an offering to God. Presumably, this is why Paul "had his hair cut off at Cenchrea" and again in Jerusalem with four others (Acts 21:22-24). One biblical scholar describes Paul's vow as "a sincere and proper expression of the ancient Hebrew faith."[1] If the Apostle Paul, who expounded grace more than anyone else in the Bible, still found such vows meaningful, we would do well to explore their potential for us in our postmodern context.

As a teenager, I made a personal covenant with God one day after reading Floyd McClung's life-changing book *The Father Heart of God*. I carefully and prayerfully wrote out a prayer, pledging myself to God and asking Him to deal with the issues of pride and selfish motivation in my life. I climbed a nearby hill on a windy day and remember well the sense of trepidation as I knelt on the grass to sign my vow. I still have that tattered piece of paper tucked away in a file, but more importantly,

---

1. E.E. Ellis, research professor of New Testament Literature at New Brunswick Theological seminary, New Jersey, in *The Illustrated Bible Dictionary* (InterVarsity Press, Downers Grove, IL: 1998).

the reality of that covenant still lives in my heart, having shaped me ever since.

The Catholic Encyclopedia defines a vow as "an act of generosity towards God." For those of us wishing to go deeper in our commitment to Christ, an exciting discovery is awaiting us in the grace of vows and covenants. These are treasures with which the Patriarchs, the Apostle Paul, and Christ Himself were clearly familiar, and yet have been all but lost by contemporary culture. We have the opportunity to give ourselves generously to God with carefully considered promises.

RENEWING THE COVENANT

> *"Consecrate yourselves, for tomorrow*
> *the Lord will do amazing things among you."*
> *(Joshua 3:5)*

121

Of course, there is no covenant that can ever supersede or add to the covenant of the cross by which we have been saved. It is better, therefore, to see any subsequent vows we make to God as acts of renewal or consecration of the covenant in which we already stand. Throughout Israel's history, there were times when the people would come together specifically to do exactly this—to renew or to ratify their covenant commitment to God (Joshua 23-24). They may even have gathered annually at the New Year Festival in order to renew their vows.

Most Christians already understand the importance of such seasons of covenant-renewal through particular times of retreat and regular participation in the covenant feast of communion. At these times, we say, in effect, "Today I am entering again into my covenant with God, which Christ initiated on the cross two thousand years ago and appropriated in my life the day I gave my life to the Lord." As we do so, we often encounter Christ afresh, because this is more than an act of nostalgic remembrance—it is a moment of dynamic promise.

Every year on our wedding anniversary, Samie and I pull an old red scrapbook down from the bookshelf, in which we have copies of the vows we made on the day we were married. We try to make time on that day each year to read those vows to one another again, apologizing wherever we have failed and thanking God for the ways we have been true to our word. It is a deeply meaningful moment— every bit as meaningful as the day the covenant began. In fact, our understanding of one another and of the promises we made on our wedding day with such naïve enthusiasm, actually grows deeper with the passage of time. This is the joy and the power of a living covenant.

As our promises go deeper with the passage of time, so the process of renewal and rediscovery becomes increasingly exciting and profound.

In the Roman Catholic and Anglican traditions, the confirmation of baptismal vows is an important spiritual rite. After confirmation, you may participate in The Eucharist, the covenant feast—the Mass. The Methodist Church has a special Covenant Service, developed by John Wesley himself, specifically to help people commit themselves afresh to the vows of faith. It begins with an invitation from the leader:

"Come, let us join ourselves to the Lord in an everlasting covenant which will never be forgotten."

The service comes to its most moving phase as each person makes a solemn vow to God:

"I do take You, O Eternal God—Father, Son, and Holy Spirit, to be my God. Be my portion. I do give up myself, body and soul, to be Your servant, promising and vowing to serve You in holiness and righteousness all the days of my life ..."

On the day we gave our lives to Christ, perhaps by walking to the front of a meeting to pray a prayer—with little idea of what we were really doing except that we needed God and He seemed to want us—we were in fact entering into an eternal covenant written in blood.

To be a Christian is to walk with God in a relational commitment every bit as serious as the covenant between a man and a woman in marriage.

In a world that has cheapened the meaning of the words we say to one another and even to God, I believe that it is time to rediscover the possibility of covenant relationship and to unlock the ultimate power of vows spoken by God, to God, and between friends with holy fear.

CHAPTER ELEVEN
CONSPIRACY

*"Christianity began in Galilee
as a fellowship of men and women
centered on Jesus Christ.
It went to Greece and became a philosophy.
It went to Rome and became an institution.
It went to Europe and became a culture.
It came to America and became an enterprise.
We need to get back to our roots."*
(Richard Halverson, former chaplain to the U.S. Senate)

Sitting staring into the flames of an open fire one night, my friend Jim (who is one of the wisest people I know) said something that has helped me ever since. He observed two equal motivations in my life: *friendship* and *vision*. I am always dreaming up new schemes and creating adventures, but if my friends don't want to join me in pursuit of the vision, I often lose my heart for it, too. Conversely, if my friends have no vision and sit around doing nothing with their lives, I quickly become bored and frustrated. But when vision and friendship marry in adventures of conspiracy and camaraderie, I am always at my happiest. Friends dreaming together—that is, for me, the dream in itself.

CONSPIRACY THEORY

If we are interested in making history and impacting the world around us, we should take a look at how this has happened in the past. In a famous course of lectures on the philosophy of history, the German philosopher Hegel outlined the two prevailing theories about how history is shaped:

- *The "World Spirit Theory"*—History is shaped by the impersonal forces of economics, dialectical materialism, or even quasi-religious "fate."
- *The "World Leader Theory"*—History is shaped by heroic and anti-heroic figures such as Alexander the Great, Karl Marx, Abraham Lincoln, Adolf Hitler, or Winston Churchill.

126

God certainly does work through the impersonal forces that shape culture, and He also raises up great leaders to impact the history of every age. But Hegel failed to identify perhaps the most potent force in human history: the catalytic effect of the "faithful minority." The anthropologist Margaret Mead, who studied cultures all over the world said, "Never doubt that a small group of thoughtful, committed citizens can change the world. Indeed, it is the only thing that ever has."

Christians should not be surprised by Margaret Mead's observation. Jesus had just three years in which to save the planet, and He did it primarily by recruiting and training a dozen friends to become a faithful minority. He did not seize political or religious power, and He often hid from the public gaze. The Son of God spent His time teaching a small group of ordinary people, and He did this primarily by sharing His life with them. This unlikely strategy turned the world upside-down and continues to shape cultures and shake the very foundations of modern life.

THE CLAPHAM SECT

In the late 1700s and early 1800s, a group of friends came together in Clapham, South London, with an extraordinary commitment to one another and to Christ. They were all wealthy and influential, but had decided to use their resources for the glory of Christ. The group, which became known as The Clapham Sect, consisted of business people, politicians, governors, clergymen, and a playwright. The most famous member of the group—William Wilberforce—was a member of Parliament. When he committed his life to Jesus at the age of twenty-six, the conversion was such a profound experience that Wilberforce considered resigning from politics altogether, but John Newton—the former slave-trader and author of the hymn "Amazing Grace"—persuaded him to keep his seat in Parliament, to fight for the abolition of slavery.

The Clapham Sect sect met in the home of a wealthy banker to conspire together for the transformation of society and the evangelization of the world. As well as fighting slavery, they worked to ban bull-fighting, improved working conditions in factories, established three major missionary societies, founded an entire country as a safe haven for refugee slaves (Sierra Leone), started schools, and gained permission for missionaries to go to India.

But members of the Clapham community paid a high price to achieve so much. Henry Thornton, a successful banker, sometimes gave as much as 80 percent of his income away. Wilberforce suffered a nervous breakdown and nearly died. On one occasion, his life was in such danger from the slave lobby that he required an armed guard. Just days before his death in 1833, Wilberforce finally achieved his great life goal: The emancipation of slaves as British citizens was passed in Parliament.

In the Clapham Sect, we see the constructive and creative power of faithful minorities, when bonded in deep friendships around a common goal, to change their world in the name of Christ.

ℭOVENANTING WITH FRIENDS

*"Promising is an extraordinary phenomenon. A promise is utterly
fragile; so easy to break, yet it can also generate bonds that last a
lifetime ... A relationship or group of any depth will, if it wants to last
through the sufferings, joys, boredoms and distractions of life, draw on
the language of promise keeping."*
(Dr. David Ford[1])

God loves to connect people in covenant relationship. We know this about marriage, but it is true of platonic friendships, too. Jesus said the world would recognize His disciples by our love for one another. Clearly there should be a depth of relationship and mutual commitment in Christian relationships that is startling to a watching world. I am not saying we should enter carelessly into widespread covenant relationships. Proverbs warns: "It is a trap for a man to dedicate something rashly, and only later to consider his vows" (Proverbs 20:25).

128

However, God does connect particular people to support and strengthen one another on the journey of life. Some friendships will come and go, but others really are for life and should be recognized and enjoyed as such. As we begin to explore Rules of Life in the next two chapters, I want to encourage you to consider whether perhaps there are others with whom God is calling you to embark in mutual commitment on this journey.

As well as the all-important covenants cut between God and the Church, there are many covenants in scripture simply between friends. Ruth makes a moving promise to her mother-in-law Naomi saying:

"Where you go I will go, and where you stay I will stay. Your people will be my people and your God my God. Where you die I will die, and there I will be buried. May the Lord deal with me, be it ever so severely, if anything but death separates you and me" (Ruth 1:16-17).

1. David F. Ford, *The Shape of Living* (Zondervan, Michigan: 2002) p. 43.

CONSPIRING WITH FRIENDS

There is no place in the Christian community for the serial monogamy mentality where each new friendship comes with a shelf-life. When a relationship gets awkward, or boring, we do not simply move on to another connection. Instead, we dare to go on a life-long journey together, through conflict and disappointment as well as seasons of mutual fascination and fun. In so doing, we "stir one another up to love and good deeds," at the very times when we might otherwise have allowed embers to die. Iron sharpens iron, and burdens are carried with empathy the extra mile. Our friendships survive seasons of vulnerability when people see our sin and somehow still choose our company and laugh at our jokes. We turn acquaintance into friendship and a few of these friendships into life-long, covenant camaraderie.

We do not measure such relationships in units of time, items of exchange, or depth of conversation (important as such things are). We measure such relationships in the shared sacraments of life—its pain, its redemption, its fellowship, its hope. In persevering, and even promising, we find friends with whom we can walk and talk in silence, "guardians of one another's solitude," as Rilke described it. "By this," Jesus said, "all men will know that you are my disciples, if you love one another" (John 13:35).

In the last chapter, we looked at the power of covenants, mentioning the fact that Methodists have a ceremony for renewing their covenant, while Catholics and Anglicans place a heavy emphasis on the value of confirmation. Such covenant commitments play an important part for many in their journeys of faith. However, as someone who was confirmed as a teenager into the Anglican Church, I can say with some conviction that without ongoing human fellowship and accountability, such vows to God are often weakened. But when we marry covenant with conspiracy, a moment of consecration to God with a clear commitment to specific people, we unlock the deepest potential of a holy vow.

People today crave such deep friendships. The most popular sitcoms of all time—from *Cheers* to *Friends*—all describe such relational groupings, where the commitment to one another outlasts every tribulation. As we make our vows to God, He calls us to work out our obedience in commitment to one another, for richer and poorer, in sickness and health. This may take the form of an extended family, a marriage, a business partnership, or even a religious Order united in a Rule of Life.

𝕷ORD OF THE RING

In the shower at the gym, I think God spoke to me. "This *Vision* book," He seemed to be saying, "is not just about the past: the words you wrote in that prayer room all those weeks ago. It's about something I want to do in the future. I want this book to be a springboard for something new."

Okay, I thought, washing my hair, *a springboard for what?*

God seemed to continue the conversation like this: "I'm calling this generation to rise up and follow me on a journey that will take you beyond anything you have yet imagined. People have been stirred by the words of 'The Vision,' but I'm challenging you to embrace something deeper than passing moments of inspiration. I'm calling you to live 'The Vision' continuously. It's time to surrender your lives to the true power of my covenant."

Then came the next bit—an idea so unexpected and forceful that it made my heart leap: "Pete. The time has come for the Honourable Order of The Mustard Seed. It's time for the vow."

Now, unmistakeably, God had my attention.

Many contemporary Christians are talking about Rules of Life: the value of carefully considered vows as some kind of spiritual compass in an increasingly confusing world.

In the shower that day, I felt I received the green light from God on the timing and also the revelation of the "Rule" He wanted me personally to pursue with some of my friends. It was to be the eighteenth century vow of Count Ludwig Nicklaus von Zinzendorf—the simple and remarkable Rule of his Honourable Order of The Mustard Seed (which we explore in the next chapter). Members of this Order wore a ring inscribed with the motto, "None live for themselves,"[2] and solemnly pledged:

- To be true to Christ,
- To be kind to people,
- To take the Gospel to the nations.

As I considered this vow, something suddenly stirred in me and I began to realize how the high aspirations of "The Vision" could be rooted in earthy realities and sobering commitment.

131

I have since wrestled long and hard with this word from God. I have studied—in fact, a group of five of us have all studied hard. Two of my friends even flew in a three-seater plane to Germany just to check out Zinzendorf's archives. We have translated original documents from ancient German and Latin into English. Throughout this fascinating process, I have prayed and questioned and allowed the dust to settle. One of the people to whom I submitted the idea was my old friend Justin Blake, who often has extraordinary insights from God. Sitting across the table from him, I shared my Post-Workout-Shower-Revelation and asked if he thought I was crazy. Was God really speaking about a three-hundred-year-old German Order? Justin cleared his throat (as he always does when he's about to say something he senses to be from God) and very deliberately removed his wedding ring. He pushed it across the table, inviting me to take a look. I could see some kind of inscription on the inside of the ring. Squinting at the tiny writing I found four words: *"None live for themselves."*

---

2. The literal translation is "no man liveth unto himself"; however, I have chosen to give it a non-gender specific translation throughout this book.

The primary pledge of the Order of The Mustard Seed had already been neatly inscribed inside his wedding ring. I gasped, and a broad grin spread across my old friend's face.

Holding the precious golden band, he now looked steadily at me: "Pete," he said, "I had Zinzendorf's vow inscribed on my wedding ring because I always believed this day would come." He paused to let his words sink in. I began to shake my head and laugh in surprise. "I always knew," he continued, "that this 24-7 movement would somehow one day give rise to a rediscovery of the power of this ancient vow." Another pause. The excitement was burning in his eyes. "Pete, it's time for the Mustard Seed," he whispered. "I, too, believe that it's time for the vow."

This book is about *The Vision*—a call to discipleship, but it is also about *The Vow*—an invitation to embrace a Rule of Life. Of course, I pray that the words of "The Vision" and the call to grow in grace continue to help you follow Jesus. But if you find yourself yearning for more, if you long to live this vision and not just read it, perhaps it is because the Holy Spirit is wanting to take you somewhere you have never been before. Perhaps as you read this book, the words that began as simple inspiration may become for you a life-long invitation echoing down two thousand years from the shores of Galilee, "Come, follow me ... Carry your cross ... Go and make disciples."

You may be at the beginning of the road of discipleship, or many years down the path, but the call is the same: to open our *hearts* afresh to the grace of God that gives birth to sacrificial living, to open our *eyes* again to see a vision of Christ and the crying needs of the world, and to open our *ears* afresh to hear the call into covenant relationship with God. This then is the voyage of the vision and the vow.

In the next chapter, we will explore the history of the Honourable Order of the Mustard Seed: its vows and the extraordinary impact this little-known Rule has had. Then, in the final section of this book, you will find an *invitation* for you and your friends to consider adopting these vows for yourselves.

132

CHAPTER TWELVE
ORDER

*"They entered into a covenant to seek the Lord the God of their fathers,
with all their heart and soul."
(2 Chronicles 15:12)*

It wasn't until the mysterious death of a Prussian officer in Amsterdam that the secret got out. Abraham von Rumswinkel had been a professional soldier stationed in Holland, but, upon his death in 1737, those searching his belongings discovered an extraordinary secret—strange symbols and documents: a golden ring with an inscription in Greek and a list of rules written in formal German.

Slowly it emerged that this ordinary Prussian officer had, in fact, been a member of an extraordinary secret Order reaching to the very highest echelons of society, right across Europe and even into the New World of America. It was hard to believe, but other members of this mysterious Order included the King of Denmark, the Anglican Archbishop of Canterbury, the Roman Catholic Archbishop of Paris, the Secretary of State for Scotland, a military general and governor of the colony of Georgia, and even an eighty-seven-year-old Indian chief called Tomo-chi-chi. The leader of the group was a well-known German aristocrat with a reputation as a religious zealot—a man in his thirties by the name of Count Nicklaus Ludwig von Zinzendorf of Saxony. The existence of The Honourable Order of the Mustard Seed had finally come to light.

The rumors spread like wildfire as the statutes of this secret society fell at first into hostile hands. A Professor Voget of Utrecht attempted to use them to discredit the Moravian missions movement expanding so rapidly under Zinzendorf's patronage. And so, reluctantly, in 1740, the Count went public with the Rules, the relationships, and the history of his Knightly Order. The truth that emerged was not sinister, but it was truly extraordinary: Some of the most powerful people in contemporary society had banded together in a solemn covenant not for self-preferment, but rather to live selflessly for Jesus Christ!

For Zinzendorf, it had all begun at boarding school ...

BEATING

"Next week," announced the school notice board, "the Count is to have the stick."

Punishments at Halle Academy for Boys, near the German city of Leipzig, were advertised well in advance to ensure a good audience and to maximize the torment of the intended victim—not that there would have been much of a problem drawing a crowd in this case. Like any child of wealth and privilege, the young Zinzendorf was resented by many of his peers and distrusted by his teachers, who considered him dangerously self-assured.

In a Pietist school like Halle, where Christian spirituality was central to educational philosophy, any trace of pride was stamped out mercilessly. And merciless it could be. Between the age of ten and sixteen, young Zinzendorf— whose father had died when he was a baby and who had been raised thus far by his grandmother—found himself regularly beaten and publicly humiliated. On one occasion, they stuck imitation donkey ears on his head and made him stand at the front of the class to be mocked. Zinzendorf stared back at the class defiantly; "This shame shall not crush me," he said in Latin, "On the contrary it shall raise me up."

For his first three years at Halle, the head teacher deliberately placed Zinzendorf in classes below his ability in order to humble the boy further. And, on the day in question—as the stick whistled and cracked repeatedly against his flesh—the boys jeered and cheered while Zinzendorf gritted his teeth and tried (unsuccessfully) to hold back the tears.

The young Count's life had already been mapped out for him in considerable detail, beginning with six miserable years at Halle. After the Academy, he was to attend university to study law, and then the young aristocrat would take a year out to see the sights of Europe and network high society before taking up his post as a Law Lord in Saxony. But right now, thoughts of higher education and state service were not exactly at the top of Zinzendorf's mind. He had to dine with professor Francke in less than an hour, and his backside still hurt like crazy.

🦋 COUNTER-CULTURE

For as long as Zinzendorf could remember, his heart had been to live for God. As soon as he learned to write, Little Lutz (as his family called him) would scribble letters to Jesus and throw them out of the window in the hope that the Lord would find them. At the age of eight, so he told his friend and eventual biographer Augustus Spangenburg, he had a crisis of faith and briefly considered that God might not in fact love him or even exist, but he soon got over it.

135

Now in the harsh world of Halle, Ludwig found solace and strength in prayer. He prayed privately, but also began to gather with other students, in lofts and any secluded place they could find around the school, to seek God and discuss matters of faith and life. As they did so, their lives increasingly matched their words. Zinzendorf and his friends had begun a quiet counter-revolution which Professor Francke eventually acknowledged was having a positive impact on the whole student community. By the time he left the school at age sixteen, Zinzendorf informed the professor that he was leaving behind no fewer than seven "churches-within-church." But the most far-reaching aspect of this mini-revival at Halle was the genesis of one particular group, formed by the ringleaders of the revival, that would last a lifetime and touch the world.

In Zinzendorf's final year at Halle, the five young leaders of the school revival got together and decided to do what teenagers have been doing in various forms since the dawn of history.

They agreed to start a band.

Had they been living in the twenty-first century, it would have been a rock band. I can imagine George Wilhelm von Soehlenthal on lead guitar. Frederick de Watteville would probably have played bass, and Zinzendorf, with his gift for poetic expression, would have written moody lyrics and dressed in black, stealing the show as a charismatic lead vocalist.

But it wasn't the twenty-first century, and the band they started was to be an order of chivalry. It was not unusual for young noblemen, who owed their position in life to traditions and social orders dating back to the Middle Ages, to organize themselves into close-knit bands with a defined purpose and an "oath of allegiance." The difference for the group at Halle was that their knightly allegiance would be sworn to Christ the King and Him alone.

136

Like all high school bands, they apparently spent more time discussing their style and their lyrics than actually performing anything. At first, their group was called "Slaves of Virtue," later "Confessors of Christ" and ultimately—by the time Zinzendorf was nineteen—it was known as "The Honourable Order of the Mustard Seed."

It is sometimes taught that Zinzendorf started the Order of the Mustard Seed (OMS) at Halle when he was fifteen. Certainly this was where the original idea for such a band began, but it took at least two years before the name, the vision, and the vow were formalized. There was a key moment of commitment and initiation—as we shall see—but this was part of a process of growth and deepening relationship.

For most high school bands, the move to university spells the end, but

Zinzendorf and his friends had touched something of God that they knew was for life. As Zinzendorf moved up to the University of Wittenburg to study law, the community stayed together by writing letters, and in the spring of 1718, they arranged to gather and formally take the vows that would bring their Order into being.[1]

PLANTING A SEED

It was a cold, dark night by the time Count Frederick de Watteville rode into town. Two drunken students were staggering down the cobbled street past Zinzendorf's lodgings as Frederick dismounted and knocked at the door. Inside the house, a roar of laughter was followed by a warm surge of familiar voices—voices that had broken from boyhood into manhood together in one long conversation. One of the voices grew louder, there was a fumbling for bolts, and the door swung open. Zinzendorf himself stood silhouetted in the doorway, grinning from ear to ear, and the two friends embraced: old friends for such young men.

137

Ushered into the warmth of the room, the five men sat in a semi-circle facing the fire, and conversation quickly turned to the matter at hand. There would be no dinner that night, as they had agreed to fast. Each one had come carrying a small pouch containing a golden ring inscribed with the Greek: "None live for themselves."

The banter soon turned from stories of Halle to the future. There was tangible excitement in the room, and yet it was imbued with an unusual solemnity. They all knew what they were here to do—the correspondence had been extensive and the discussion deep—there were vows to be made that would last a lifetime and propel each one of them out into the vast ocean of life under the captaincy of Christ.

Two of the group were destined for the courtly responsibilities of aristocracy.

1. The exact date on which the Order formally started in unclear. This sequence follows J.R. Weinlick's *Count Zinzendorf* (Abingdon Press: 1956) and is supposed by Gerhardt Reichel in *Der "Senfkornorden" Zinzendorfs*.

All of them would soon come of age. Years of dreaming, scheming, playing, and praying together had convinced them that these friendships were for life and that their lives were for Jesus. Perhaps they knew the stories of mariners binding themselves to the ship's mast at the approach of a storm, determined at all costs to see their families and their native lands once more. They knew that it was time to bind themselves to one another and to Christ in a covenant that could hold them true and carry them through every storm the future might bring.

Zinzendorf rose from his chair and, turning his back to the fire, looked at each member of the group: "Brothers, we know why we are here," he said, holding aloft a golden ring glinting in the light of the flames.

"Tomorrow we will make our covenant, but tonight let us pray."

The murmur of prayers began, ebbing and flowing as each voice explored another dimension of the vow they were soon to make. They prayed for God's help to be true to Christ in the face of temptation, confessing their sins easily in one another's hearing. Frederick threw another log on the embers, and as the flames flared up, Zinzendorf cried out that God would consume him, too, with the fire of holiness. Soon they were praying for greater love for their fellow students, their families, and for unity in the body of Christ. And thus their prayers turned outwards for distant lands and unknown tribes ignorant to the love of God. They mentioned missionaries by name who had visited Professor Francke at Halle. They pledged to use all the gifts of wealth and influence at their disposal for the "conversion of the heathen" and the salvation of the Jewish people.

Eventually the prayers subsided, as did the flames in the grate, and the men sat silently, enjoying the stillness for many minutes before retiring to bed.

When they came down the next morning, none of them was surprised to see that Zinzendorf had been up all night, conducting one of his prayer vigils. Without breakfast to eat, they turned quickly to the ritual for which they had been preparing so long.

After prayer and a little discussion of each aspect of the covenant, they stood, one at a time, and with little emotion, each one made their solemn vow to God. Next they knelt down as Zinzendorf placed the ring on their fingers, laid his hand on their heads, and prayed. The ceremony had taken minutes, but it was to last a lifetime.

When all was done, they ate a hearty feast—breaking bread and drinking wine—to celebrate the covenant of their friendships: The Honourable Order of the Mustard Seed had been planted in good soil.

The Moravian Bishop Herbert Spaugh would later summarize the covenant they made that day as follows:

1. To be true to Christ;
2. To be kind to all people;
3. To send the Gospel to the world.[3]

The members of the Mustard Seed Order had managed to distill the very essence of the Gospel into just three commitments—an achievement made all the more extraordinary by the fact that they were teenagers at the time. And although they lived three hundred years ago, their vow is still utterly relevant, profound, and compelling. They may have been young, but they were also deadly serious in their intentions. On one document, a member promised "rather to lose his life, than to depart from the faith."[4] Given the turbulent history of bloody sectarian violence that still stalked Europe at that time, such a pledge was no vain sentiment.

In reading this story, it is hard not to be inspired by these disciples-of-their-

---

3. Herbert Spaugh, "A Short Introduction to the History, Customs and Practices of the Moravian Church," EverydayCounsellor.com.
4. A.G. Spangenbert, *The Life of Nicholas Lewis Count of Zinzendorf and Pottendorf,* translated L.T. Nyberg (Bath: 1773) part 1, chapter 2, section 10, footnote 1.

times, and by their commitment to live and stand by the vow they had made. However, in the back of our contemporary Christian minds, we may hear a little alarm bell ringing: "Surely all this talk of vows, of oaths, of secret societies is out of date? Relevant to their time, but not to ours? A dangerous and unnecessary addition to the Word of God? The stuff of cults and sects if placed into the wrong hands?"

Jesus had the greatest respect for the law of God and lived a life that upheld it to the spirit and the letter, but He showed enormous reluctance to suggest additions to it. When asked by a legal expert to summarize the Law, He replied: "Love God with everything you've got, and love others as much as you love yourself. That's it" (Matthew 22:37-40, paraphrase). When, after His resurrection, He stood before His friends and could have commanded them to do anything, He simply told them to take the good news to the world and make disciples wherever they went (Matthew 28:18-20).

140

These then are the three most fundamental commands of Christ: love God, love people, and proclaim the good news. Zinzendorf and his companions had not added anything to the Word of God or the commands of Christ. They simply re-stated the essentials of faith given us by Jesus Himself: to love God, love our neighbors, and fulfill the Great Commission.

THREE-DIMENSIONAL DISCIPLESHIP

In a complex world, the vow of the OMS simplifies and clarifies the call of Christ. To be all that God created us to be, and to do all that Christ has called us to do, the disciples of Jesus must constantly live on all three planes of reality: loving Christ, our neighbors, and the nations.

The relationship between these three vows is also vital. Some people are true to Christ in their morality and worship, yet they seem unconcerned about world mission. Others are passionate about evangelism and the nations, yet they are really unkind to people in the way they go about it. Still others are kind and tolerant to everyone they meet and would hate to ever offend anyone, but in so doing, they have lost sight of the Great Commission to preach and the Great Commandment to love God more than man. But, when all three of these vows come together in a single life, you have something balanced, beautiful, and powerful for God.

The Order's greatest influence was upon Zinzendorf himself. When he arrived back in his native Saxony, after graduation and traversing Europe recruiting likeminded members for the Order, Zinzendorf graciously agreed to let Moravian refugees establish a community on his land. He would later admit that he had felt bound by his oath of kindness "as a knight of the Order of the Mustard Seed" to offer them assistance.[5] However, it was a life changing decision.

In welcoming the last remnant of the old Bohemian Brethren Church, Zinzendorf initiated a chain of events, which became one of the most dramatic and far-reaching moves of God in modern church history.

141

- Unwittingly, his decision fulfilled the century-old prophecy of the great educationalist Comenius, who had prayed that God might preserve a "hidden seed" of faithfulness in the Moravian church that would one day grow into a great tree.[6]
- It led to the dramatic visitation of the Holy Spirit at Herrnhut in 1727, which became known as the "Moravian Pentecost."
- It launched a 24-7 prayer watch which lasted continuously for a hundred years.
- It was pivotal in John Wesley's transformation from a broken and disillusioned man into one of the most powerful revivalists Britain has ever known.
- It flowed outwards in a missions movement that was one of the

5. Weinlick refers.
6. Jan Amos Comenius was a Moravian bishop regarded as many as the founder of modern education. *LIFE* magazine even dubbed him as "the inventor of childhood."

first organized attempts to take the Gospel to the nations, and reached to America, Greenland, South Africa, the West Indies, and many other nations.

SELFLESS SERVANTS

Zinzendorf wrote a letter to Chief Tomo-chi-chi, leader of the Creek people, who had become a Christian and even a member of the Mustard Seed Order. Such Native Americans were patronized as mere primitives by the Count's contemporaries, yet in his correspondence with Tomo-chi-chi, the man who had been accused of arrogance at Halle, signed himself off as "your slave, Zinzendorf."[7] The noble-blooded Count had learned that he was nothing without Christ and had been commissioned to serve, to send, to be kind, to be loyal. Even the name of the Order speaks of humility. Their first adolescent title—The Slaves of Virtue—had sounded self-righteous. Their next incarnation as The Confessors of Christ sounded somewhat heroic. But in maturity, the friends settled on the simplest and subtlest identity of all—the insignificant mustard seed of negligible faith that somehow grows into a great tree (Matthew 13:31).

142

As members of OMS stepped down from their positions of privilege to be kind to all people and true to Christ, who gave up heaven itself, they defied the very fabric of the prevailing social system.

Charles Spurgeon, the great British preacher, said of Christ: "His glory was that He laid aside His glory, and the glory of the Church is when she lays aside Her respectability and Her dignity and counts it to Her glory to gather together the outcasts."[8]

One day, the Church will be known not for her pomp and power, but for her humility, her service in the name of the servant King, to the least, the lowest, and the most despised. We will become a people whose value system points to the very humility, loyalty, and kindness of God. On that day, Christ's bride will finally

---

7. The letter is found in a collection entitled *Texts of Mission* by Wittig. Translation by Markus Lägel.
8. Cited in Philip Yancey's *Rumors of Another World* (Zondervan, Michigan: 2003) p. 198.

be ready to marry her groom at the wedding feast of the Lamb:

Your attitude should be the same as the Church, who
being in very nature Christ's beloved
did not consider her call to rule and reign
as a thing to be grasped
but became a simple nobody
indistinguishable from the poor
utterly human
nothing special.
And being found in appearance as a loser
she continued to choose downward mobility
to the ultimate dead-end
of anonymity, failure, and even martyrdom.
Therefore
God swapped her overalls, covered in blood, mud, and grime,
for the most beautiful bridal gown of all time.
He placed a ring upon her calloused finger
and gave her His name—the one above all others—
that when she walks down the aisle,
her crimson dress as white as snow,
her bridal procession should number thousands upon thousands
from every tribe and tongue
their hearts overflowing with joy
as the trumpet sounds
and the wedding feast begins
forever.

"Come now, let's make a covenant, you and I,
and let it serve as a witness between us."
(Genesis 31:44)

*"And this is the sound of the underground;
the whisper of history in the making;
foundations shaking;
revolutionaries dreaming once again ..."*

the vision and
the unw

THENESIS

CONSPIRACY IS BREATHING ONCE AGAIN . . .

CHAPTER THIRTEEN
RULE OF LIFE

My friend Carl and I decided to join a gym. But because joining a gym is generally easier than using one, we also set ourselves a challenge to see who could achieve the flattest stomach by Christmas. The race was on ...

It was September, but we already had tickets to see a stand-up comedian in London on December 17 and agreed that this comedy night should be the three-month deadline for our six-pack challenge. And so, glancing nervously at the pregnant curve beneath each other's T-shirts, we shook hands and settled upon a big-money, cash prize: twenty pounds.

Three months of intense rivalry and good-natured goading ensued as two erstwhile slobs began pounding, pumping, running, and crunching several times a week, determined to win that Big Cash Prize and the vain-glory of a washboard physique.

The days got shorter, and all too soon, December found me gazing forlornly in the mirror, contemplating the (previously ambiguous) merits of taking steroids. I would soon be forced to expose my moderate paunch to the rounded laughter of friends and—adding insult to so much injury—the embarrassment was almost certainly going to cost me a cool twenty notes.

Determined to make defeat as dignified as possible, I decided that rather than handing Carl boring cash, I would buy him something that would commemorate his moment of glory. Preferably something that he would truly hate.

Our comedy night began with Carl and me standing topless in a crowded noodle bar in central London, exposed to the hilarity of our friends and the evident dismay of slurping diners. Standing next to Carl Barkey's rippling stomach, like Winnie the Pooh taking on Terminator, I tensed, scrunched, and sucked every abdominal muscle. But Carl's toning triumphed by unanimous consent. Not even one measly sympathy vote from a whole bunch of my so-called buddies. Visibly deflating, I replaced my shirt as quickly as possible, shook Carl's hand, and presented him with a large, brown envelope, the contents of which had set me back precisely twenty pounds. Carl Barkey looked at me quizzically and pulled from the envelope an elegant certificate assuring him that he was now the proud sponsor of a very small fish at the London Zoo. What was more, a plaque would soon be erected to tell the world that it had been named after him.

As far as I know, he still hasn't visited little "Two-Pack Barkey," and he'd better hurry, because they don't live long.

So much energy and vision had been released in a couple of couch potatoes by a mere handshake and the prospect of that final ritual. Through a simple commitment, we had found discipline to pursue our best intentions in our daily lives over a period of three months. Joining the gym was not enough. It was a good start, but we needed our own rules, true to our characters and friendships, in order to attain the goal of better physiques.

In just the same way, having joined the Church, our high ideals may well prove insufficient without a practical plan for ongoing inspiration and discipline, "for what I want to do I do not do, but what I hate I do" (Romans 7:15).

The commitment Carl and I made brought focus, accountability, and even joy to the process of *physical* transformation. Many Christians, for similar reasons, find it helpful to commit themselves to a Rule of Life, in relationship with others, whereby they find focus, accountability, and joy in the lifelong journey of *spiritual* transformation. Paul exhorts: "train yourself to be godly," precisely because transformation is not automatic, but requires discipline and hard work. However, as he goes on to imply, spiritual discipline gains for us infinitely more than a six-pack stomach and a fish in the local zoo, "for physical training is of some value, but godliness has value for all things, holding promise for both the present life and the life to come" (1 Timothy 4:8).

As we seek to grow in discipleship, personal vows—like those of Zinzendorf—can be a powerful tool, helping us to break addictive cycles of behavior in our lives, to shake off laziness, and to grow in the likeness of Jesus. Zinzendorf's vow, to live unselfishly for Christ, for others, and for the world, went on to shape his entire life and transformed a middle-ranking German aristocrat into one of the great heroes of the Christian faith.

- It was because he had promised to be *kind* that he allowed refugees to live on his land, contrary to the culture of his time.
- It was because he had given himself to world *mission* that he turned a localized revival into the greatest missionary movement of his generation.
- It was because he had pledged his allegiance to *Christ* that he lived with his eyes fixed upon the end of the race and built something eternal with his life.

From these three tiny mustard seeds of faith—mere words planted by a naïve and unhappy schoolboy—a great tree grew to touch the nations (Luke 13:19).

WHAT IS A RULE OF LIFE?

A Rule of Life is a set of principles and practices we build into the rhythm of our daily lives, helping us to deepen our relationship with God and to serve Him more faithfully.

If creeds are *what* we believe and Christ is *why* we believe, a Rule is *how* we seek to live out that faith, day-to-day as disciples in the power of the Holy Spirit. Individuals, communities, and even secular programs for personal development are increasingly adopting such Rules of Life as a strategy for fostering intentional change and growth.

TRANSFORMATION

There's a great Sufi story about a seeker who was traveling the earth in search of God—examining every religion and looking carefully at different ways of life. One day, she arrived at a monastery and asked a monk, "Tell me, does your God work miracles?"

He chuckled and replied, "Well, it all depends how you define a miracle. Some people think that it is a miracle if God does the will of the people. But here in this community, we think a miracle is when people do the will of God."

God's power to transform our motivation is one of the most exciting dimensions of the Christian experience and has always been one of the great, sparkling proofs of the Gospel. At age eighteen, I went to Hong Kong to work for a remarkable mission among the poor. Day by day, I saw lives transformed by the power of prayer and community. I watched heroin addicts set free by Jesus. I saw Him nurturing hardened Triad gang members, whose bodies were often covered in tattoos of strange gods, and gradually these men became dignified and gentle.

People came to us like emaciated little birds, and Jesus fed their souls so they could feed their own bodies. He put muscles back on bones, squared sagging shoulders, inhabited vacant eyes, and straightened the spines of the ashamed. An old prostitute, whose veins had collapsed through a lifetime of heroin injection, found peace and purpose, tending flowers and caring for children.

The Russian novelist Leo Tolstoy said: "Everybody thinks of changing humanity and nobody thinks of changing himself." I admit that I went to Hong Kong in order to change the lives of the poor, but quickly realized that I was the poor one needing to be changed.

In Asia, I found myself surrounded by people who were blatantly so much more like Jesus than I was that I became increasingly embarrassed to be me. For the first time in my life, I realized that my instincts were almost always entirely selfish, that my conversation was punctuated with insecurity, and much of my humor was simply unkind. It also dawned on me that my gifting didn't impress God. He could talk through a donkey if He so desired. I began to realize in my heart what I had known in my head for a while: that God is interested in my character—the real me, including the secret phobias and drives of my inner life.

I began to cry out to God to change me. I knew there was no doctor, no shrink, no preacher, no person on earth who could re-wire me the way I needed to be re-wired, and so I talked a lot to God. I had one day off a week, and by the end of my time in Hong Kong, I was spending most of that day alone in a small tin hut, hidden from the bustling city, often weeping and asking God again and again to "change my heart or take me home."

151

I returned to England unaware that God had begun to answer my prayers, but those who knew me well all saw that I had changed. I was still a long way from perfect, but my conscience had been re-sensitized to the subtleties of sin. I found that I was liking people more, I was less harsh in my speech, more comfortable in my own skin, and much hungrier for God. Nothing but the Gospel of Christ can change the DNA of a person's soul in such a way.

When the Gospel liberated my friend Paul from a spiraling drug habit, he found he had the money to buy his mother a Christmas present for the first time in years. He chose that gift carefully and gave it with such joy that his mother was truly moved—just one in a million snapshots of the Gospel at work.

I have another friend who is highly successful in business, intelligent, well connected, and very wealthy, yet he is hungry—desperately hungry—to meet with

God, more and more, in worship. His priorities defy material logic.

Every single one of us carries hurts that only Jesus can heal, sins that only His blood can cleanse, and a hunger that He alone can fill. Rules of Life enable us to appropriate the transforming power of the cross repeatedly in our daily routine, our crazy schedules, our base instincts, our career choices, our remorse, and our recreation.

THE A-B-C OF LIFE

Rules of Life can provide us with the A-B-C for a deeper walk with God:

- *Authentic*—A Rule helps us to live consistently with our convictions. Mountain-top experiences will never transform our characters without daily discipline, covenant community, and a set of personal values. A Rule can therefore be a *compass* in confusing times.
  > E.g. the Rule of the Celtic Northumbria Community is a simple and profound covenant to *availability* and *vulnerability*, which they describe as "an ethic for Christians and other aliens in a strange land."
- *Balanced*—A Rule enables us to develop a balanced, sustainable, and enjoyable rhythm of life. By mapping out the different dimensions of our faith in a few simple principles and practices, we are better able to balance the multiple demands of our diaries, in a life that is well lived and not driven by inner insecurity and outer expectation. If we are to stay faithful in the long haul, without blowing up or burning out, a Rule of Life may well be the metronome we need to keep us moving forward "in step with the Spirit" (Galatians 5:25).
  > E.g. the Benedictine Rule emphasizes the daily

balance between work, rest, and prayer lived out in community.

- *Centered*—A Rule calls us back continually to the place of prayer and worship as the life-giving spring from which everything else flows. A Rule can cut across the self-complicating tendency of Christianity, keeping us grounded in Christ's simple presence. A Rule is therefore a *plumb line* measuring everything we say, think, or do against the example of Jesus.

  > E.g. St. Francis gave us the key to his Franciscan Order when he wrote: "Every day I find so much sweetness and consolation in meditating upon the memory of the humble witness of the Son of God, that should I live till the end of the world, there would be little need of my hearing or meditating upon anything further in the scriptures."[1]

When Samie was first pregnant, the doctor gave her a long list of foods and activities she should avoid, exercises she should do, supplements she should take, and check-ups she should attend. She diligently followed every rule. Why? Because she loved the child she was carrying and wanted him born healthy and happy. These rules were not oppressive to her—they were life-giving! The word *rule* conjures up images of school and dreary regulations. But when we describe a Rule of Life, the word also carries its other meaning of a straight edge for measuring and drawing lines. In this sense, a Rule of Life is an instrument that enables us to keep boundaries and to measure our spiritual progress.

OCK AND RULE

Many of the men and women God has used most powerfully over the last two

---

1. Legend of Perugia, 99.

thousand years in every Christian tradition have lived according to a Rule of Life. Sometimes their Rule was not explicit, but more often, it was set out carefully and followed diligently. Some of these saints developed their own Rules, while others pledged themselves to existing Orders and communities.

Rules have been the heartbeat of life for saints from St. Francis of Assisi to Mother Teresa, for great reformers from John Wesley to William Booth, for preachers from Charles Finney to Billy Graham, for mystics from Teresa of Avilla to Thomas Merton, and for theologians from Augustine to Bonhoeffer.[2] All these people (and countless others in every walk of life) came to a critical moment in their lives when they chose to make a covenant, to follow a spiritual Rule of Life that would serve them as a compass, a metronome, and a plumb line for every other thing they did from that day onwards. In the light of this impressive list of advocates, it is surprising that so few Evangelicals and Charismatics currently practice this powerful tool for personal growth and a deeper walk with Jesus.

154

But a Rule of Life is not just a tool for spiritual giants. In fact, it is especially useful for ordinary people with jobs, college assignments, or kids to feed—people who are trying to make sense of Christ's call to discipleship in the modern world. Many people develop aspects of a Rule unwittingly. For instance, they might say grace before meals, pray diligently at bedtime, and undertake an annual retreat. They recognize that these activities are all useful disciplines helping them to grow in grace, but it has never occurred to them that they are instinctively exploring elements of a Life Rule.

Jesus was highly relational. His approach to ministry was primarily organic and interactive rather than didactic and mechanistic. However, He was also very focused and intentional about everything He did.

It is important to live intentionally, to think clearly about the vision and rhythm we desire to pursue. Developing a personal Rule, living by it, and covenanting with God—and ideally also with friends—can bring lifelong impetus, intentionality,

2. During the second Great Awakening in America, the ministry of Charles Finney (1792-1875) brought hundreds of thousands of people into the kingdom of God. On September 11, 1850, Finney preached a farewell sermon entitled, "The Christian's Rule of Life," proposing the use of 1 Corinthians 10:31 as the simplest of all Rules.

and accountability to all we do and—more importantly—the way we do it. Provided such a solemn vow is carefully and prayerfully undertaken, it can also undoubtedly be the beginning of a journey that will take us into unimagined depths of intimacy with God.

𝕵 BOAT IN A STORM

I live near the sea and love to go watch surging waves pounding against the rocks and exploding into the sky on a stormy day. Like the ocean, the world today is volatile—heaving and hurling itself against landmarks of the past. These are dangerous times for disciples of Christ. In a handful of years, the Information Revolution has shrunk the world to the size of a modem, claiming victims and victories indiscriminately. Atheistic existentialism has impoverished us, scientific discovery is outstripping ethical wisdom, multinationals are holding nations to ransom, trust is breaking down, the battle lines have been drawn between radical Islam and Western democracy, and, on the fringes of the fray, stands the Church we love, like a stuttering prophet or a dignified old lady with Alzheimer's disease. It hurts me to say it, but it is sadly true. Under such conditions, increasing numbers of people are losing their desire, or ability, to belong to a local expression of Church, and many have lost their faith altogether.

155

We must all find ways of riding out the raging oceans of our time, and instinctively, we tend to adopt one of two survival positions: resistance or resignation.

Resistance—The first response to the storm of change is to stand like a vast breakwater on the beach, allowing the waves to shudder through our timbers, but remaining unmoved and resistant to change. *Standing firm is all that matters.*

Resignation—The second response is to surrender to the waves, like a piece of driftwood, allowing the currents of life to carry us helplessly wherever they will. *Staying afloat is all that matters.*

But there is a third response open to us, which is vastly more creative and exciting than either hopeless resistance or helpless resignation. We can fashion boats. Not identical boats. But we can create vessels from the raw materials at our disposal, and these may just carry us across the ocean to lands we dream to see. We can no more conquer the times in which we live than a boat controls the sea. Vast forces—both angelic and satanic—bigger than any individual are at work in the world. This is no time for heroic charades. But a Rule of Life, constructed from the raw materials of the revelation and relationships that God has given us and bound together in covenant commitment, can enable us to hold a steady course through the waves and to harness the power of the elements as we go.

At a time of vast cultural transition, as we try to make sense of church and faith and ethics, I believe that Rules are a particularly useful tool, helping us to navigate a course between cynicism and fanaticism and to find the patterns of chaos like a ship riding the waves.

BUILDING OUR OWN ALTARS

"Sacrifice fuels the fire
of victory in their upward eyes ..."

Doug E. Ross is a twenty-six-year-old DJ who once spent a summer as a missionary among the clubbers of Ibiza. With the rest of the 24-7 team, he adapted himself to a nocturnal rhythm, going to bed as the sun rose and surfacing at lunchtime for breakfast. At night they would hit the streets, praying, partying, and helping those who were off their faces on drink and drugs. It was an exhausting way to live, and the team quickly discovered that an afternoon siesta was almost essential in order to last out the night without using drugs like everyone else. But Doug would often sacrifice his siesta to go help someone lug PA gear around the island or to quietly meet up with a contact from the night before. He didn't make a big deal out of it. He didn't complain about feeling tired. He just quietly slipped out of the villa on a little mini-mission from God while others were sensibly dozing.

This kind of unnecessary sacrifice has always distinguished God's friends. When the time came for Abraham to part company with his nephew Lot, he could so easily have called the shots and demanded the fertile valley as his domain, leaving Lot to pay his dues in the desert highlands. Abraham was older and wiser—it was his right to strike the deal. But instead, he let his nephew choose the territory, saying, "Is not the whole land before you? Let's part company. If you go to the left, I'll go to the right; if you go to the right, I'll go to the left" (Genesis 13:9). It's a touching insight into the character of the man God named as His friend.

God loves to bless His kids. Many good things are ours by right. But as we mature, we may exercise the right to waive our rights and sacrifice good things for the best of others (Romans 12:1). As we "lay down our rights and our precious little wrongs," we come to resemble the selfless Savior more and more. No one will ever force us to make such sacrifices. By definition, no one would have that right. But without such a heart, our spiritual growth will be stunted. We'll be like bonsai believers, perfectly formed miniatures of the people we could become in Christ— all potential and little power.

Lot chose to leave his godly old uncle camping in the wilds, to raise his family in the buzzing cities of the temperate Jordan plain. Doubtless he wanted the blessings he had seen Abraham enjoy, but he didn't want to endure the wilderness. Lot wanted his uncle's wealth and favor without the discomforts of a nomadic existence. Or perhaps he chose the city because the happiest years of his life had been in Ur before the death of his parents sentenced him to spend the rest of his childhood wandering with his uncle in the desert. Perhaps some childish voice inside him simply associated the conurbation with comfort and home. Whatever the reason, Lot chose the city and the grassy valley, leaving his uncle to live in the hot and dusty desert.

The biblical account reveals an interesting insight into Lot's character: Never once did he establish his own covenant with, or his own altar to, God. Lot was like so many Christians today, who want the blessing of God without the sacrifice. They see all that God has done in other generations, or even in the lives of their own leaders and mentors, but they expect to experience similar power without enduring the same pain. They are eternally glad that Christ sacrificed Himself for them, but they are not willing to make relatively small sacrifices for Him. They want discipleship without discipline, freedom without a Rule, the power of Christ's resurrection without a share in His suffering (Philippians 3:10).

Abraham allowed Lot to choose the easy option, and God also allowed Him to live a comfortable and compromised life in Sodom, as He allows so much compromise within His Church today, for a while at least.

When judgment eventually fell on the city, Lot escaped, thanks only to the intercession of his righteous uncle. Although he was saved, it was "only as one escaping through the flames" (1 Corinthians 3:15). After all those years, during which Abraham's household continued to multiply, Lot failed to bring anyone but his two unmarried daughters out of the city. Even his wife died for disobedience. And though Lot and his daughters were saved, it was only "by the skin of their teeth." From then on, Lot lived a rather pitiful and twisted existence—a man who had been saved, but never built his own altars of unnecessary sacrifice.

God longs to make nations of us. He has called us to be faithful and fruitful through sacrifice and covenant. But many Christians never build their own altars; they spend their whole lives surfing the blessing and revelation granted to others. They are saved, but "only as one escaping through the flames," taking little with them into eternity because they never sacrifice more than they have to.

We have all traveled with Abrahams—people who are blessed by God. Such people are good to be around because their "cup overflows" onto us. But reflect on the sacrifices they have made along the way, the altars they have built, the faithfulness and kindness they model. Sooner or later, we have to establish our own households of faith, building our own altars and establishing new covenant relationships.

MATURITY AND THE EXTRA MILE

"The Vision" talks about a lifestyle that "scorns the good and strains for the best." We see such a sacrificial heart in saints down the ages, from Father Abraham to Doug E. Ross. Most Christians understand the importance of sacrificing sin—laying down wrong relationships or destructive habits in order to receive greater wholeness. But as we grow up in grace, we may also sacrifice things that are not sinful—good things for the best of others. This is what Jesus means by going the extra mile. This is what Samuel means when he says, "To obey is better than sacrifice" (1 Samuel 15:22). Oswald Chambers says: "The greatest enemy of the life of faith is not sin, but good choices which are not quite good enough. The good is always the enemy of the best ... Many of us do not continue to grow spiritually because we prefer to choose on the basis of our rights, instead of relying on God to make the choice for us."[3]

159

In 1948, Billy Graham called his team together in Modesto, California, where they developed a Rule of Life that was later nicknamed "The Modesto Manifesto." It related specifically to the areas of greatest vulnerability to a high-profile evangelistic ministry such as theirs: money, sex, honesty, and relationships with the local Church. On that day, Billy himself established a rule never to meet, travel, or even eat alone with a woman other than his wife Ruth. You can imagine how difficult it must often have been to obey that rule in a lifetime of traveling and ministering. There must have been many times when the rule seemed petty and even a little legalistic. In some ways it was unnecessary; McDonald's with an aging pastor's wife was hardly going to cause a man like Graham to stumble. But the

3. Oswald Chambers, *My Utmost For His Highest* (Barbour Publishing, 1995).

fruit of such "unnecessary" sacrifice over so many years has been a solid marriage and a ministry that has outshone any hint of scandal in over five decades.

The key to being blessed by God like Abraham is to obey the voice of God sacrificially (Genesis 26:4-5). Peter tells us that God gives the Holy Spirit "to those who obey him" (Acts 5:32). First we obey, and then we are blessed. Submitting to a Rule of Life is a wonderful and very practical way of building our own altar to God and of establishing our own covenant relationships. In such sacrifice, we show that our hearts are for the Giver more than they are for the gifts, which He pours so profusely upon us.

In perhaps the most selfish and independent generation that has ever lived, the call to submit ourselves to the accountability of Rules and community can seem anathema. But this is the very time when Christ's counter-cultural disciples could rise up in obedience and willing sacrifice, vowing that "no one shall live for themselves," but for Christ Himself, for others, and for the world.

The Christian author, Rick Joyner, who is himself a member of an ancient Order called the Knights of Malta, says this: "Just as Count Zinzendorf, the true father of modern missions, created the Order of the Mustard Seed, which touched and inspired men like John Wesley to release a spiritual fire in the earth that created the first Great Awakening in America and Europe, I think that the church is in desperate need of groups who will join together to press beyond the state of modern Christianity as it is generally found in most of the world. Call these 'elitist' groups if you want, but we need them to call all Christians to higher standards of faith and life."[4]

Of course, in any Rule of Life, there are dangers:

- There is the danger of pride, should members of an Order begin to consider themselves holier than others.
- There is the danger of legalism, should we lose the heartbeat of

love and grace and begin putting our faith in the rules, which, by themselves, are just "filthy rags" (Isaiah 64:6).

- There is the danger of heresy, should we add to the demands of the Gospel. The Pharisees did this with excessive regulations that ring-fenced the Law. A Christian Rule is always an essence of, never extra to, the Gospel. As St. Stephen of Muret said: "No Rule is absolute except that of the Gospel."[5]

St. Francis freely admitted that his Rule was nothing more nor less than obedience to the Gospel of Christ. "No one showed me what I was to do, but He, the Most High, revealed to me that I was to live according to the form of the Holy Gospel."[6]

Similarly, the three vows of the Order of the Mustard Seed were simply Zinzendorf's prayerful response to the Greatest Commandment (love God) and the Great Commission (Go ...). You may choose to adopt this Rule for yourself, and we will be exploring it in the rest of this book. Or you may prefer to develop your own Rule of Life, based on the principles outlined here.[7]

161

RULE OF THE FOOL

"The Lord has called me into a new way of simplicity and humility ... So I prefer you not talk to me about any other Rule ... nor recommend any other ideal or manner of life than that which the Lord in his mercy has revealed and given to me. He told me I am to be a new kind of fool in this world."
(St. Francis of Assisi, Mirror of Perfection)

St. Francis was one of the greatest saints ever given to the Church, and his "Rule of the fool," in all its simplicity, turned the world upside-down. It never occurred to Francis to compare himself to the lukewarm congregations of his day. He

---

5. C.H. Lawrence, *Medieval Monasticism* (Longman Publishing Group: 1984).
6. *The Testament*, cited in Murray Bodo's introduction to *365 St. Francis of Assisi* (Fount: 1987) p. xix.
7. See Christine Sine's book, *Living on Purpose*. Also, find out about contemporary orders such as Taizé, The Northumbria Community, Richard Foster's Renovare Rule, or Mike Breen's Order of Mission.

never even measured himself against his friends—his band of fellow radicals. For Francis, the only standard was Jesus Christ. Having been commissioned by God to "go repair my church which is falling into ruins," Francis simply obeyed for the rest of his life. In the process, he upset countless people and broke many rules and every convention of the time, but in so doing, he "returned to the gospel with such force that it shook the entire world."[8]

As God commissions us to rebuild His ruined Church once again, perhaps He will establish new communities, new movements, new Rules and Orders, like those of St. Francis and Count Zinzendorf, helping us return to the Gospel simply and forcefully in our generation, too. If we will live out of this center—our eyes fixed on Jesus and our lifestyles radically consistent with His—then who knows? The world might shake once again.

8. Jim Wallis and Joyce Hollyday, *Cloud of Witnesses* (Orbis Books, New York, NY: 1994) p. 6.

CHAPTER FOURTEEN
RHYTHM FOR LIFE

"There is a tide in the affairs of men,
which, taken at the flood, leads on to fortune;
omitted, all the voyage of their life
is bound in shallows and in miseries.
On such a full sea are we now afloat.
And we must take the current when it serves,
or lose our ventures."
(William Shakespeare—Julius Caesar, iv iii, 217)

On June 26, 1999, at twenty to six precisely, Fran Healey struck the first chord of his song "Why Does It Always Rain On Me?" and as he did so, the heavens unexpectedly opened over the fields of the legendary Glastonbury Festival. Big fat raindrops sizzled onto the sun-scorched earth, and festival goers began dancing and laughing for joy. Exquisitely, the song had captured a moment in time, and unexpectedly, the festival anthem belonged to a little-known band from Scotland called Travis. "Something magical happened," Healey would recall.

The following week, the whole nation seemed to be singing their song. Previous Travis records had reached numbers forty, thirty-nine, and thirty-eight in the charts respectively, and the band joked that it was going to take another thirty-seven songs to reach the top. But that was before it rained at Glastonbury. Suddenly "Why Does It Always Rain On Me?" jumped into the top ten, and its accompanying album went on to sell three hundred thousand copies on both sides of the Atlantic. For eight years, Travis had worked hard with frugal success, but at twenty to six on Saturday, June 26, 1999, a passing rain cloud turned their futures to fame and fortune.

The message of this book may mark such a passing rain cloud for you. Certain moments in our lives really are more important than others, and the decisions we make during these events can shape the history of years to come. The Lord may be calling you (as He is calling me) to consecrate yourself to Him in the form of a vow: a conspiracy of friends, a mustard seed of faith, a Rule of Life. If so, then He will be speaking to you through these pages, but also in other ways. The message of this book may be converging with other parts of your life and focusing your desire for depth upon the issue of covenant. But you may feel differently, sensing that it would be premature or simply unnecessary for you to make such a covenant right now. This vow is not right for everyone, and timing is important for all. It mattered, to the minute, when Travis played that song. It matters what week a baby is born. It matters what month a couple make their wedding vows.

> *"There is a time for everything, and a season for every activity under heaven: a time to be born and a time to die, a time to plant and a time to uproot ..." (Ecclesiastes 3:1-2)*

PREPARED TO PROMISE

One of the most enjoyable aspects of pastoral ministry for Samie and me has always been preparing people to enter into the covenant of marriage. Over the years, we have noticed that loved-up couples are often in a massive hurry to marry, rushing toward the altar to say their vows because waiting seems unbearable. And yet, until such lovebirds have weathered a few problems and disagreements, they are never ready for marriage, and our pastoral duty has often been to apply the brake pedal, no matter how unpopular it makes us at the time!

In the making of any covenant—be it that of marriage or a Rule of Life—preparation, consultation, patience, and courage are vital.

My mother once drove a stick shift car at seventy miles per hour in second gear for half an hour. It was a hot day, and with the windows down, we didn't hear the screaming of the engine until it was too late. Eventually smoke began to pour from the overheated engine, which was damaged beyond repair. Everywhere I go, I meet people in a similar state: They have generally been traveling for a while on God's freeway—often at considerable speed—but their engines are screaming for change, threatening to explode unless they shift to a rhythm of life that is internally slower, more sustainable, and yet surprisingly, more powerful, too.

UNFORCED RHYTHMS

These people are categorically not looking for the superficial solution of God's Next Big Thing—a new Christian fad to keep them going a little longer. What they want—in fact what they need—is a far deeper rhythm of spiritual and social interchange, rooted in simple obedience to Jesus. "Are you tired?" He asks. "Worn out? Burned out on religion? Come to me. Get away with me and you'll recover your life. I'll show you how to take a real rest. Walk with me and work with me—watch how I do it. Learn the unforced rhythms of grace. I won't lay anything heavy or ill-fitting on you. Keep company with me and you'll learn to live freely and lightly." (Matt. 11:28-30 MSG)

165

The "unforced rhythms of grace" come to those who bind themselves to Christ—who walk with Him and work with Him.

We live in a world that associates rest with the absence of work and freedom with the absence of rules. But when a heart stops working, it is not resting—it is dying! There is work to do—a yoke of obedience—but with Him, it is "easy." There is a burden to carry, but when we carry it with Jesus, it becomes "light." When we find ourselves "burned out on religion," it is time to rediscover the heartbeat of Christ's presence, to stop working *for* Him and start working *with* Him. Such moments of spiritual "gear-change" can be healthy and happy events in the maturing process, provided we get the timing right. Maybe you are considering such a change right now:

- Perhaps you are facing a moment of practical transition—like Zinzendorf's graduation from Halle to Wittenburg—and it is causing you to evaluate both your past and your future.
- Perhaps you yearn to live radically for Jesus, yet your spiritual journey is leading you away from the easy answers you once espoused so passionately. You are maturing in grace, and you've experienced your share of disillusionment, but as you grow up, you don't want to grow cynical and lose the vision and passion of child-like faith.
- Perhaps there are people with whom you sense a deep connection, and although you don't yet know why, you do know that the journey henceforth is meant to be together.
- Perhaps you realize that you are driving fast without a road map and God has been calling you for quite some time to build depth into your life, as well as breadth, to address the long-term issues of the way you live and not just what you achieve.

GROWING UP, GROWING OLD

For my part, I have decided that I want to grow old with friends asking myself the same three questions each day:

- How can I be true to Christ today?

- How can I be kind to people today?
- How can I play my part in taking the Gospel to the nations today?

I don't know what ecstasies and agonies the future may bring, but I do know that the dream for the rest of my days, whatever may come, is to be consistently true to my Savior, kind to my neighbor, and committed to the nations of the world. This is—for me—what it means to be Christ-like, what it means to be a disciple, what it means to be a faithful lover of Jesus. For others, it may mean something else, but for me, this will do. I do not intend to become any more prescriptive than this, lest Rules detract from the heartbeat of my relationship with Jesus, who is my reason for building this altar of praise. Knowing the usual fate of my good intentions, especially the ones I make when I think I am standing firm (1 Corinthians 10:12), I have decided to bind myself to the Gospel in this way through a solemn vow.

"Why should we bind ourselves to loving God, submitting to a religious rule; why take the vows?" asks Raniero Cantalamessa, preacher to the papal household.[1] "The answer," he says, "is that in a moment of grace you were drawn to God, you loved him and ... dreading the thought of losing him because of your instability, you 'bound' yourself to guarantee your love from every possible change."

Because I love God less than I want to, and distrust myself entirely, I am launching out on this journey with friends who are more than friends. Together, we will find ways of exploring the meaning of these three simple vows year by year for the rest of our lives, going deeper in understanding, growing simpler in knowledge, allowing the Holy Spirit to speak to us about each one in new ways at different times.

Seasons will come and go, and the terrain ahead is sure to change, so our vows will mean different things at different times. The oath of allegiance to Christ

---

1. Raniero Cantalamessa, *Life in Christ, a Spiritual Commentary on the Letter to the Romans* (The Liturgical Press, Minessota, 1990), p.127.

will sometimes mean withdrawing in prayer and worship for a period of hidden intimacy with Him. But then at other times, this same vow will propel us out of the cloisters to find the one we serve amongst the poor and to receive fresh revelation from the rush and bustle of His world. Sometimes, Christ's call to kindness may require of us a radical response to global injustice, but at others, it may mean shrinking the horizon on such grand concerns, just to take a long vacation eating ice-cream with our neighbors' kids. The call to the nations will cause us all to live as pilgrims, moving with the pillars of cloud and fire; for some, it may well mean passports and visas, while for others, it will mean personal witness on the home-front in the world of work.

Sadly, I know that I will fail most days in some way or other—most often I suspect in the realm of simple kindness. But as I keep my eyes on Jesus, there is grace to change. As Paul puts it, "we, who with unveiled faces all reflect the Lord's glory, are being transformed into his likeness with ever-increasing glory" (2 Corinthians 3:18). Day by day, as I outwork my vows, God's grace will subvert my selfishness so I can think big enough to disciple nations, small enough to care for my neighbor, and deep enough to be loyal to my Lord for life.

When I fail, please grant me grace. And should I succeed—so that one day they say, "He was faithful, kind, and he loved the Gospel"—give God glory for His extraordinary achievement, and remember a simple mustard seed planted by Zinzendorf, almost three hundred years ago, which grew into a tree that is now bearing fruit once more. Climbing in its ancient branches with my friends, perhaps we shall see the world from a different perspective, enduring storms in winter and enjoying summer's sweetest fruit, because we are rooted in Christ through all life's changing seasons.

CHAPTER FIFTEEN
ETERNAL LIFE

A self-important teacher of the Law was, once again, trying to trip Jesus up: "What do I need to do to get eternal life?"

Jesus sighed, knowing the answer was already blatantly clear in the very Law of which this man was supposed to be an expert. Sure enough, the teacher provided the answer to his own question without hesitation: "'Love the Lord your God with all your heart and with all your soul and with all your strength and with all your mind,' he said, and, 'Love your neighbor as yourself.'"

Smiling in mock surprise, Jesus addressed the teacher as if he was a pupil: "You have answered correctly," He said. "Do this and you will live" (Luke 10:25-28).

Zinzendorf and his friends had decided to chart the course of their lives entirely by just three guiding stars: love for God, love for their neighbor, and thus—inevitably—love for the lost as well. In so doing, they had correctly identified the very essence of what, according to scripture, it means to live well, fully, and even eternally. "Do this," Jesus says, "and you will live."

You may by now be considering the idea of following in the footsteps of Zinzendorf and his friends by adopting the three vows of the Order of the Mustard Seed as a personal Rule of Life. You may even be thinking about taking the vow with certain close friends as a modern day expression of the Mustard Seed Order. But what does such a commitment look like in practice? In this chapter, as we draw to a close, I want to explore the implications of the three vows in more detail. However, because I have expounded on the first promise (to be true to Christ) already in various parts of this book, I'm going to focus more on the second vow, kindness, and the third, mission to the nations.

1. LOVING GOD: THE VOW TO BE TRUE TO CHRIST

"This is the first and greatest commandment."
(Matthew 22:38)

Author Mike Bickle often talks about the importance of putting the first commandment first. At the start of this book, we explored the fact that to be true to Christ is to know Him as Friend, trust Him as Savior, and obey Him as Lord.

- We know Him as Friend by coming to Him in intimacy, sitting regularly at His feet, and walking with Him day by day.
- We trust Christ as Savior by embracing His grace, even when we feel too bad to be saved, too broken to be healed, or too boring to be used.
- We obey Christ as Lord by leaving our nets, building our own altars of unnecessary sacrifice, and obeying His command to "Go" and make disciples.

2. LOVING OUR NEIGHBOR: THE VOW TO BE KIND TO PEOPLE

"Love your neighbor as yourself."
(Matthew 22:39)

I was still reeling from the shocking revelation. Bright shards of sunlight were cutting through the cigarette smoke of the bar, which was packed with students laughing and drinking their way through the lunch break.

The event had seemed such a great idea—advertised all over campus as "Grill a Christian"—an opportunity to throw every imaginable accusation or complaint at a panel of God Squad regulars in the raucous belly of the bar at lunchtime.

There had been palpable excitement from those pagans keen to throw a gullible Christian or three to the lions once again, but the only believers stupid enough to take part in the panel were myself and a couple of friends, and we weren't even students here. To me it had sounded like fun, but not anymore ...

I'd arrived on campus that morning, spent time in prayer with the organizers, and then, as we walked across to the bar, they finally gathered the courage to tell me the one thing I really needed to know ...

"We're, um, really glad you could come," Sam said, glancing at me sideways. "Actually, it's amazing they've allowed us in again after last time ..."

"Why, what happened last time?"

171

Sam looked at me and laughed nervously: "It was a couple of years ago, and there were—a few problems," he replied, clearly wishing he hadn't embarked on the conversation in the first place. "They sort of, like, banned us from ever doing this again."

"Wow!" I said. "How come?"

"A local pastor came in to do the panel thing like you're doing, and a girl asked a question about abortion."

"Okay," I said, "so what happened?"

"Well, the pastor told her that it was the same as killing your own baby—murder in the sight of God. I guess he said it kind of passionately, and the thing was ..." We were almost at the doors and clearly needed to talk before going in. Sam turned to face me before blurting out the truth: "The girl who asked the question had just had one—she'd just had an abortion. She was pretty upset, and she ..." Sam's voice trailed away for a moment, and then he whispered, "she went away from our event and tried to kill herself."

I imagined the guilt, confusion, and fear the girl must have felt as the pastor's verdict of "murder" echoed the self-condemnation in her heart. With a sense of foreboding, I realized that this was likely to be far more than a good-natured lunchtime debate about the relevance of religion. Suddenly I was terrified of entering that bar. The girl herself might even be in there.

Once we were inside, the microphone crackled and whistled, someone fiddled with the sound desk, and the crowd grudgingly hushed. Some people were annoyed that their drinking time was being interrupted by the God Squad; others were staring intently at the three of us perched precariously on bar stools at the front like the three wise monkeys. I scanned the crowd, picking out the occasional bright-eyed Christian, utterly conspicuous amidst the sea of diffidence and defiance. The guy on the microphone invited the first question. There was a protracted pause, and then, reluctantly it seemed to me, a girl holding a pint of Guinness raised her other hand.

"What," she asked, with a cold smile, "is the Christian view on abortion?" It was as if two years had passed in two seconds, the same question still echoing around the same crowded bar. The room fell silent, every eye fixed on the three muppets at the front. My heart was racing as I took the mic and stood. I could feel hatred from some of the eyes, just waiting to be offended by the words I would surely say.

The Scriptures assure us that when we find ourselves on trial, the right words will be given to us, and in that moment, as I stepped terrified from my bar stool, it happened. Suddenly I knew exactly what to say and how to say it.

I looked around the room and then slowly knelt down before them.

The crowd became motionless. Just the curls of cigarette smoke and the shards of light. No other movement. Eyes that had been apathetic moments earlier were now looking at me like I was crazy. The angry eyes seemed surprised. The occasional Christian smiled encouragement. My heart was pounding, and my knuckles were white as I clenched the microphone to my lips.

Two words: "I'm sorry."

The bar was utterly still: It was the absence of movement, but perhaps it was also the presence of peace. Suspended animation.

"I'm here," I continued, "to apologize for all the times people like me have been more bothered about dogma and position than loving people the way Jesus did. Some of you here know what I am talking about." I noticed a few nods. The girl at the back had put down her Guinness. "I've been told what happened here in this bar two years ago, and I want to say I'm sorry. Christians can be wonderful people, but sometimes we are also just incredibly unkind in the ways we relate and communicate. It's pretty ironic really," I attempted a grin, "when you look at the example of our founder." No one laughed. "I guess I'm here today to say a single word: 'Sorry.' I'll understand if you don't want to hear anything else."

I waited on my knees, unsure what to say or do next. And then it happened: Someone, somewhere, began to clap. Others joined in. They didn't clap for long, but they really did clap, appreciatively, generously, and gently. Absolution more than applause: forgiveness from a community offended and wounded by the uncaring administration of Christian truth.

I often get such situations wrong. I am sometimes the one who commits the unkindness, the one who hurts the very people I've been sent to help. But on this particular occasion, God gave me the key to unlock a little healing. The questions flowed freely after that, good and honest questions without bile or barb, and we attempted to answer with goodness and honesty, too. And in our honesty, we had to say some things that we knew would be unpopular because they contradict the prevailing culture, but we attempted to do so with gentleness and humility. Several times we remembered to pause, to probe the questioners for their own thoughts or experiences. We remembered that the love of God is always kind.

I really like the fact that the members of the Order of the Mustard Seed chose to commit themselves to kindness and not merely loving everyone. I say "merely," because it sometimes seems harder to be kind than to love. "In love," we say terrible things to one another, and all the talk of "loving the lost" seems to mean so little in practice. We say we love our enemies while we sue them in court or kill them in battle. Sometimes kindness—one of Paul's definitions of love in 1 Corinthians 13—is more costly to dispense and more beautiful to receive, than the thing we call love.

THE KINDNESS OF CHRIST

I reckon that Jesus cooked breakfast for hungry fishermen primarily because He was kind. He prioritized children because He was kind. He cared about the loneliness of His mother even on the cross because He was kind.

Jesus was kind to everyone except those who were self-righteous (Matthew 23). Even at His arrest, He stopped to heal the ear of the servant attacked by Peter. Jesus was always especially kind to women who had messed up their relationships.

- He chose to reveal His identity to the woman at the well who had been through five divorces.
- He refused to condemn the woman caught in the act of adultery.
- And then, on Easter morning, He appeared first to Mary Magdalene, probably a former prostitute.

I wonder if it was because He remembered the things people had said about His own mother as He was growing up. There must have been gossip and innuendo surrounding the suspicious circumstances of His conception out of wedlock, and perhaps such painful memories primed Jesus to be especially tender toward women who were being used or accused by men.

It is often in our own experiences of sin and hurt that we find the grace to be kind. The word "vulnerability" comes from the Latin, literally meaning "woundability." The wounds of suffering can callous our hearts to the needs of others, but they can also bruise and soften us to care more, to listen with greater understanding, and to live with deeper kindness (2 Corinthians 1:4-5).

GRAFFITI ON THE WALLS OF THE CHURCH

Perhaps it needs to be stated clearly: Our commitment to kindness must begin with the house of the Lord. Some of us have far more grace for non-Christians than we do for our own brothers and sisters, mothers and fathers in the faith. Our Orders and Rules do not replace the local congregation. The entire Franciscan Order was built upon the call to rebuild the Church, precisely because it was in ruins. Zinzendorf saw his groups not as an alternative to other Christian communities, but rather as "church-within-church," and worked hard to gain acceptance for the Moravian denomination from the Anglican Archbishop of Canterbury.

So many of us live our lives like graffiti on the walls of the Church. We know that we belong in the congregation of the faithful, but we long for her to change in so many ways. It's true that we do not always express our dissatisfaction as kindly as we should. Maybe there is, coursing through our veins, too much of John the Baptizer's blood and not enough of John the Beloved's for us to hold our peace and play the game the way we should.

But we can't abandon the Church in order to impact society, not least because Jesus is jealous for His bride. He is sick of the superhero syndrome that thinks another brand, another man, can somehow save the world, thus divorcing revival from renewal, truth from mercy, revolution from evolution, the hope of the kingdom from the community of Christ with all her flaws. Jesus is calling His entire Church to rise up in sacrificial obedience. It's Him who is extraordinary, not us. The challenge—the vision—is always to fix our eyes exclusively on Jesus, the hope of the world and the lover of the Church.

Christians are often spectacularly kind, and this is the greatest evidence of Christ in our midst. Jesus said, "Greater love has no-one than this, that he lay down his life for his friends ... This is my command: Love each other" (John 15:17). Each time we dare to take the bread and drink the wine, we commit ourselves again to revolutionary relationships and a violent forfeit of personal preference in the interests of others.

I'm sick of all the excuses we make for the state of our churches. I'm bored with all the talk, the programs, the strategies for growth, the latest all-conquering theories on evangelism. That stuff's a decoy. Show me how to love. Right now I'm not too bothered about meetings, the preaching, the music. I'd trade the lot of it for something else. Lately I've been longing more than anything else to belong to a community that is purely and simply deeply kind.

And then I look in the mirror.

> *"Be kind to each other in your homes. Be kind to those who surround you.*
> *I prefer that you make mistakes in kindness rather than that you work miracles*
> *in unkindness. Often just for one word, one look, one quick action,*
> *and darkness fills the heart of the one we love."*
> *(Mother Teresa in a letter to her Sisters of Charity)*[1]

We can't limit our kindness to our fellow believers. We are also called to "be kind to those who surround" us, who know little or nothing of Christ and disagree with our convictions, as I discovered powerfully that lunchtime in the student bar. It has often been suggested that one of the things Christians and non-Christians have in common is that we all hate evangelism. Ironically, it may well be when we stop "doing" evangelism and start loving our neighbors for their company rather than their scalps, that the Church will grow in breadth and depth. This Gospel

1. Eileen Egan, *Such a Vision of the Street, Mother Teresa* (Sidgwick & Jackson, London: 1985) p. 362.

virus never did spread from brain to brain, but rather from person to person, friend to friend, down long corridors of time and mutual exchange, through minefields of offence and great orchards of honest love. It is in such terrain that Christ moves freely and at ease. It is in such conditions that the contagion spreads.

3. LOVING THE WORLD: THE VOW TO TAKE THE GOSPEL TO THE NATIONS

Kahlil Gibron's book *The Prophet* describes kindness that turns to stone because it does nothing but gaze at its own reflection all day. Jesus has commissioned us to turn our lives and our churches outwards to take His love to those who have never heard the Gospel.

As we have seen, the commission to take the Gospel of Christ to the nations flows from a three-thousand-year-old covenant. God promised Abraham that He would "make his descendants as numerous as the stars" and that through them, "all nations on earth will be blessed."

In fulfillment of this covenant, Jesus commissions us to multiply as a blessing to the nations. For Zinzendorf, this meant mobilizing missionaries to distant lands and unreached people groups. In April 1731, the young Count met an African slave from the Danish West Indies who told him of terrible conditions facing the plantation workers. He returned to Herrnhut in July and shared the story. In response, two of the Moravians volunteered to go to the West Indies, even if it meant selling themselves into slavery. On August 21, the following year, the first two missionaries left on foot for Copenhagen. On October 8, they finally set sail for America, and five days later, they arrived at last in the West Indies. The Moravian missionaries worked hard, but, having given up everything for these people, after eighteen months, they had gained just one convert.

Seventeen more Moravians arrived to join them in June 1734, eight of whom died of yellow fever. Undaunted, eleven more missionaries arrived in February, and four of them died in their first two months. In 1735, most of the survivors were forced to return to Herrnhut, three of whom drowned in a ship-wreck. The whole enterprise must have seemed like the most costly failure imaginable.

However, in 1736, there were signs that the tide might be starting to turn and a little while later, Zinzendorf traveled to visit the colony. Unaware of recent encouragements, he turned nervously to his traveling companion as their ship landed and said: "Suppose the brethren are no longer here; what shall we do?"

"In that case," replied his friend, "we are here."

In fact, they discovered a church of eight hundred people, sown in the blood of so many martyrs. In such stories, we see the practical outworking of Zinzendorf's vow to send the Gospel to the nations. At the heart of The Order of the Mustard Seed was a living, Christ-centred, mission-minded, practical faith. In fact, the very first item of the written version of their Rule states: "This then is the aim of our work in the whole world: that we reach the hearts of all for the sake of the One who gave His life for our souls."[2]

SPHERES OF INFLUENCE

When an occupying army moves into a nation, they take authority over a vast landmass by gaining control of the economy, the military, the media, and the schools.[3] In the same way, the missionary commission sends us out to influence and exercise Christ's authority in every sphere of society. A commitment to the Great Commission is just as likely to propel us into the realms of business, teaching, or the media, as into more overtly spiritual activities like Bible translation, pastoral ministry, or digging wells in the developing world. The earth is the Lord's and everything in it, and He calls us to make disciples of every nation, blessing every tribe, every culture, in His name.

2. "Rules of the Honourable Order of the Mustard Seed," published Budingen, 1740, Section I. Tr. from an original in the Moravian archives at Herrnhut by Markus Lägel, paraphrased into modern English.
3. Loren Cunningham, *Making Jesus Lord* (YWAM Publishing: 1997).

THE GREAT DIVIDE

It's high time we detonated the insidious myth of the sacred/secular divide that labels certain activities "spiritual" and everything else "worldly." The Bible teaches, and the Jews understood, that the only truly secular thing is sin.

Like the Israelites, the ancient Celtic Christians had a buzzing, holistic faith that found Christ in every aspect of life and worshiped Him in the mundane as well as the mystical. It was life-affirming and earthy. In fact, one of my favorite Celtic prayers begins, "I make this bed in the name of the Father, the Son and the Holy Spirit"! Our God is out there in every aspect of mundane existence. He's behind the headlines, on the air-waves, between the lines of print, inspiring artists, anointing cancer research, and feasting with the poor.

The danger of modern worship styles is that we exalt Jesus so high on Sunday, with our hands aloft and eyes shut, that by Monday morning, when our eyes are wide open and our hands are hard at work, He's out of sight and out of reach for another six days. Theologian Clarence Jordan describes the problem brilliantly: "Jesus has been so zealously worshipped, his deity so vehemently affirmed, his halo so brightly illumined, and his cross so beautifully polished that in the minds of many he no longer exists as a man. He has become an exquisite celestial being who momentarily and mistakenly lapsed into a painful involvement in the human scene, and then quite properly, returned to his heavenly habitat. By thus glorifying him we more effectively rid ourselves of him than did those who tried to do so by crudely crucifying him."[4]

179

God is inviting us to re-possess the real world and not to flee from it. We are the salt of the earth, but anyone who eats a whole plate of the stuff gets sick. We are the light of the world, but no one stares at the bulb. He's sending us out, small and insignificant as we are, to redeem music, medicine, the arts, and education, to reclaim the streets, to scatter heaven lavishly in every prison, theater, bar and lecture hall. And He calls us to do all this with uninhibited kindness.

4. From the introduction to *Cotton Patch Version of Luke and Acts* by Clarence Jordan, cited in Jim Wallis and Joyce Hollyday, *Cloud of Witnesses* (Orbis Books, New York, NY: 1994) p. 71.

AN INVITATION

*"You are standing here in order to enter into a covenant
with the Lord your God, a covenant the Lord is making with you
this day and sealing with an oath ..."*
(Deuteronomy 29:12)

We began this book with a vision, and we conclude with an invitation to find a rhythm and a Rule for life, embedded in community and expressed in a vow.

Specifically, I believe God is calling forth a modern day rediscovery of the Mustard Seed Order, which impacted so many lives so profoundly in the past and could do so again for the glory of His name.

CYMBROGI

The ancient Celts had a term, *cymbrogi*, which means, "companions of the heart." I believe God is calling us to gather our cymbrogi, as did Zinzendorf, to covenant ourselves to one another and consecrate our lives to obey the Greatest Commandment and to fulfil the Great Commission.

As you read this book, the eyes of the Lord "range throughout the earth to strengthen those whose hearts are fully committed to him" (2 Chronicles 16:9). He is looking for those people with passion and courage even in such a selfish and cynical age: "children of God without fault in a crooked and depraved generation, in which you shine like stars in the universe" (Philippians 2:15-16).

Just imagine, for a minute, what might happen if such cymbrogi—cells of the Order of the Mustard Seed—were planted in thousands of churches and in every Christian tradition, bringing faith and renewal. We could start a contagion of kindness and grace, modeling authentic, balanced, and Christ-centered lifestyles of discipleship. We could catalyze a fresh movement of mission and justice in every sphere of society where Christ is not known. It would not be a new organization or brand, but rather the loosest of networks outworked locally—for all its global potential—in the small, the quiet, the mundane, and the real. While we dream of great trees, let us plant small seeds of friendship and imperfect faith.

Perhaps such covenants could galvanize faithful minorities to make history in the name of Christ once again. Faithful minorities in politics, like Zinzendorf's Order and and the Clapham Sect. Faithful minorities in the Church, like the early Franciscans and Bonhoeffer's Confessing Brethren. Faithful minorities in the marketplace, like those first followers of Christ.

184

Perhaps it's an impossible dream, but this is what I am longing to see: presidents and priests, rock stars and sporting personalities, journalists and scientists, living their lives on earth as citizens of heaven and servants of the King.

For the rest of my life, I will be wearing a ring on my finger, and it will remind me each day of a simple, solemn vow I once made with my cymbrogi. When I shake hands with a stranger, I will remember. When I clench my fists in anger, I will remember. When I handle money, I will remember.

These hands will age. There will be wrinkles and liver spots. The veins will one day soon look like rivers, I am sure. But the ring will remain on my finger as a reminder of the vow a younger man made—a circle of gold as a promise of purity for an imperfect soul, a circle of eternity for a life strung together, from day to day, like rosary beads. I hope to wake each day and see the ring. And one day I will wake in the great Amen, and hear the words, "Well done, my good and faithful servant. Yes, my friend, I knew you." The ring—merely a metallic token of eternal grace—will have vanished from my finger, left behind in the realm of dust. Vows and rings will be no more.

TAKING THE VOW

I have attempted to establish some principles for making and keeping covenants, and as we draw to a close, we will now look at some practical guidelines for all those wishing to enter into the vow of The Honourable Order of the Mustard Seed:

- *Preparing* to take the vow—The Vision
- *Making* the covenant—The Vow
- *Maintaining* the vow—The Voyage

1. THE VISION: PREPARING TO TAKE THE VOW

185

In this book, I have shared a vision, which people must appropriate for themselves. If you should choose to do this in the form of a vow, it is vital to count the cost carefully and to prepare yourselves diligently (Proverbs 20:25).

The old monasteries and Orders to this day apply a lengthy "novitiate" period for prospective members. During this time, novices explore the vows and prepare themselves for the rigors of their Rule to see if it is truly right for them.

The Order of the Mustard Seed evolved slowly over several years until eventually Zinzendorf and his friends settled on a vow that was both true to the Gospel and appropriate to their lives. Jesus spent forty days fasting in the wilderness before launching out in public ministry and a whole night in private prayer before choosing the twelve disciples. In cutting a covenant with friends, we must be careful not to manipulate, hurry, or hype the obligation, but rather allow the relationships to mature naturally to the place of deeper commitment.

The book of Deuteronomy advises us very practically about making vows. Those still living in their parents' homes should avoid taking such a promise without parental consent (30:3-5). Those who are married should talk the commitment through with their partner first (30:6-8). On the basis of this advice, I would discourage people from entering into The Order of the Mustard Seed before the age of consent or if their marriage partner opposes the commitment.

PRAYER AND STUDY

If you are planning to take the vow alongside others, gather together, in the build-up to the ceremony, to discuss the meaning of each of the three vows you are preparing to make. During this period, it is also strongly advised that you take time to examine your heart in the light of each promise, confessing to God and one another areas of selfishness and sin that the Holy Spirit highlights as you do so.

Just as Jesus prepared Himself for big decisions and key moments of His life by withdrawing in order to fast and pray—so as you build up to your vow, you may choose to go on a retreat or pilgrimage to a place of personal spiritual significance or to conduct your own night vigil in prayer. Immediately prior to the ritual, you might like to prepare yourselves spiritually by fasting for at least a day.

As well as preparing prayerfully, the group will need to make practical decisions for the ceremony, agreeing upon a significant date and time for the covenant to be activated and allocating responsibilities for the day.

SYMBOLISM

Consider an outward symbol of your heart commitment. The Nazirites shaved their heads and burned the hair as an offering to God. Jonathan gave David his cloak. Zinzendorf inscribed rings. Partners in business and marriage sign an official document. You might even consider designing a tattoo—should your conscience permit—to be worn for life by the members of your covenant community. In an age that rarely understands the permanence of promises, a modest tattoo could be an effective reminder of the seriousness and longevity of this pledge.

Those wishing to become members of the Order of the Mustard Seed should wear a ring inscribed with the phrase, "None live for themselves." Such rings should be chosen and inscribed in advance of the ceremony and symbolically placed on the finger at an appropriate moment in the ritual.

2. THE VOW: MAKING THE COVENANT

Once the wording of the vow has been agreed upon, its implications explored, the cost carefully counted, and an appropriate ceremony been planned, the covenant may be cut.

LITURGY

You will need to appoint a "facilitator" for the ceremony. This could be a person who has already taken the vow and is thus initiating others into the Order, or it could be a recognized leader within the group of novitiates. Consider the exact words you will use to make your pledge. As with wedding vows, this is not a time for spontaneity. The vow of the Mustard Seed Order, as you know, involves three promises: to be true to Christ, to be kind to people, and to take the Gospel to the nations. Here is a suggested liturgy (but please feel free to adapt it or even to develop your own version entirely):

2.1 INTRODUCTION
- The facilitator welcomes the group and summarizes the purpose of the gathering.
- The group shares a time of worship and open prayer.

- Each novitiate speaks, explaining to the group why he or she is wanting to take the vow.
- A short biblical exposition of each of the vows is offered. In between each one, a prayer may be said, asking the Holy Spirit to help the group in this area.

2.2 THE PERSONAL VOW TO GOD BEFORE ONE ANOTHER

Facilitator: [Name], have you prepared yourself carefully, prayerfully, and accountably to take this vow?

Novitiate: I have.

Facilitator: [Name], do you understand that the promise you are about to make is for life and that it will not make you any more righteous in the eyes of God than you were on the day you first believed?

Novitiate: I do.

Facilitator: Then I invite you, in the presence of these witnesses, to consecrate yourself to God now in a solemn vow.

The novitiate then makes his or her vow, for example:

- Fool that I am, I pledge my life to be *true to Christ* in the grace of the Holy Spirit for every year of life the Father grants me. So help me God.
- Weak as I am, I pledge my life to be *kind to people*: to see Christ in others, to serve Christ in others, and to show Christ to others in the joy of the Holy Spirit to the glory of the Father. So help me God.
- Small as I am, I pledge my life to *the Gospel of Christ*, in the

power of the Spirit, that He might be loved in every tribe and every nation in this generation to the glory of the Father forever more. So help me God.

2.3 PRESENTATION OF GIFT

The novitiate is presented with a gift that is symbolically meaningful to them as they begin their journey. This may be done by the facilitator, another novitiate, or by a close friend or mentor. The group may gather around and pray for the new member.

2.4 THE CORPORATE VOW TO ONE ANOTHER BEFORE GOD

Once all novitiates have made their personal vows to God, the whole group stands in a circle (numbers permitting):

Facilitator: The Lord Jesus, who calls us to follow and commissions us to bless the nations, also commands us to love one another. We love because He loved us first. Today, as we consecrate ourselves to God, we also covenant ourselves to one another. No one is to live for themselves any longer, but for Christ, for one another, and for the lost.

Novitiates: As the Father loves us, let us love one another.
As Christ serves us, let us submit to one another.
As the Spirit intercedes for us, let us support one another.

Facilitator: "Let us hold unswervingly to the hope we profess, for he who promised is faithful. And let us consider how we may spur one another on toward love and good deeds. Let us not give up meeting together, as some are in the habit of doing, but let us encourage one another—and all

the more as you see the Day approaching"
(Hebrews 10: 23-25).

Novitiates: We do not live for ourselves, but for Christ.
We do not live for ourselves, but for one another.
We do not live for ourselves, but for the nations.

2.5 PRESENTATION OF RINGS

A ring may then be placed on the finger of each novitiate by the person standing next to them in the circle. The person placing the ring on the finger may say: "Christ in you, the hope of glory" (Colossians 1:27). On receiving the ring, the novitiate may say: "Yada" (a Hebrew word meaning "to serve faithfully in accordance with the covenant").

Facilitator: Let us worship Jesus Christ. "He is the image of the invisible God, the firstborn over all creation. For God was pleased to have all his fullness dwell in him, and through him to reconcile to himself all things, whether things on earth or things in heaven, by making peace through his blood, shed on the cross. Once you were alienated from God and were enemies in your minds because of your evil behavior. But now he has reconciled you by Christ's physical body through death to present you holy in his sight, without blemish and free from accusation—if you continue in your faith, established and firm, not moved from the hope held out in the gospel" (Colossians 1:15-23).

2.6 CELEBRATION OF THE COVENANT

Conclude the proceedings with a celebration of the new day that has dawned.

Perhaps the best way of doing this is with music and a feast. You may like to incorporate the covenant meal of bread and wine in this feast, should your tradition permit.

3. THE VOYAGE: JOURNEYING WITH THE VOW

Of course, taking the vow is just the start of a lifelong journey. As we proceed, we must continually scan the hard-drive of our lives for the lethal viruses of superiority and pride. The covenant we have taken should not—I suggest—be secretive, because this could incubate a culture of control. If anything, you should keep the Order open to new members as the journey unfolds. Members are free to initiate others into the Order with the same rigor and consideration they themselves applied to the process. However, although exclusive secrecy is unhelpful, discretion is important, protecting you from pride and the jealousy or suspicion of others. Transparency, rather than publicity, is the key.

It is vital that you establish mechanisms for ongoing support, growth, grace, restoration (when members fail), and renewal. Each member may well find it helpful to find their own spiritual director willing to guide them through their commitment. Or you may agree to meet regularly to explore some aspect of the Rule and to honestly share your struggles, insights, and encouragements. Perhaps you could arrange to reconvene annually on the anniversary of your vow to renew your commitments. If you have made your vow privately, it is even more important to develop such moments and find mentors.

We have established a website called *www.mustardseedorder.com* as a meeting place and a resource for members of the modern day Order. On this site, the three dimensions of the Order are explored in some depth, with new articles being added regularly. Through the Internet, we can offer some loose connection and central resources for all those on this journey together, particularly providing teaching material that explores the challenges of living out our three vows in the real world. The site also carries remixes of "The Vision" and a forty-day study guide to accompany this book.

In years to come, there may be many thousands of such groups that have joined themselves in the Honourable Order of the Mustard Seed, but we have deliberately chosen not to build a brand, an infrastructure, nor any centralized control for the movement. The Lord has led us simply to release this righteous invitation to the nations, scattering the seed to grow wherever the soil has been prepared.

> *"I have much more to say to you, more than you can now bear. But when he, the Spirit of truth, comes, he will guide you into all truth ... He will bring glory to me by taking from what is mine and making it known to you."*
> *(John 16:12-14)*

After just three years of public ministry, Jesus left imperfect disciples without any specific structure and only the counsel of the Spirit, yet these ordinary people went on to re-write history. Like those first disciples, we, too, have committed our lives to Christ's three great commandments. As we embark on this journey "leaning not on our own understanding," we can be sure that He will lead us—as He has always led His people—a step at a time, into all truth.

In his epic poem about King Arthur and the Knights of the Round Table, Alfred Lord Tennyson offers one of the most moving depictions in modern literature of loyalty and lordship expressed in loving covenant.

"Arthur sat
Crown'd on dais, and his warriors cried,
'Be thou the king, and we will work thy will
Who love thee.' Then the King in low deep tones,
And simple words of great authority,
Bound them by so strait vows to his own self,
That when they rose, knighted from kneeling, some
Were pale as at the passing of a ghost,
Some flush'd, and others dazed, as one who wakes
Half-blinded at the coming of a light.

But when he spake and cheer'd his Table Round
With large, divine and comfortable words,
Beyond my tongue to tell thee—I beheld
From eye to eye thro' all their Order flash
A momentary likeness of the King ..."
(Lord Alfred Tennyson)[1]

193

Tennyson's poem echoes an eternal theme which has been both the vision and the vow of every age: of Anna the widow and Wilberforce the politician, of Francis of Assisi and Teresa of Calcutta, of Peter the apostle, Zinzendorf the Count, Rilke the poet, and Bonhoeffer the pastor. By the grace of the King, their vision has become ours, and so with them and with our cymbrogi, we, too, now bow the knee and speak the words Eden longs to hear:

"Be thou the king, and we will work thy will
Who love thee."

---

1. Alfred Tennyson, Ed. J.M. Gray, *Idylls of the King: The Coming of Arthur* (Penguin Classic, USA: 1989).

And thus:

> *"From eye to eye thro' all [our] Order flash*
> *A momentary likeness of the King."*

A momentary likeness of the King. Surely that is all we ever wanted.

"Let us begin, my brothers,
For up to now we have done but little."
(Last words of St. Francis of Assisi[2]*)*

2. Celano, *First Life*, 103, cited *365 St. Francis of Assisi*.

WWW.24-7PRAYER.COM

A meeting place for the international 24-7 Prayer community.

TRAINING:

To find out more about transformational training courses in Europe and America exploring the three vows of the Mustard Seed Order, write to *training@24-7prayer.com.*

WWW.MUSTARDSEEDORDER.COM

A website connecting and resourcing the Order of the Mustard Seed worldwide, including a study guide to accompany this book, music downloads of "The Vision," articles by leading thinkers exploring what it means to be true to Christ, kind to people, and committed to Christ's global mission in contemporary culture.

WWW.24-7TITLES.COM

Find out more about other 24-7 Prayer publications, including all the latest resources.

the Vision and
the Vow

THE VISION
BY PETE GREIG

....

So this guy comes up to me and says, "What's the vision? What's the big idea?" I open my mouth, and the words come out like this ...

The vision?
The vision is Jesus:
obsessively, dangerously, undeniably Jesus.

The vision is an army of young people.
You see bones?
I see an army.

And they are free from materialism—
they laugh at 9-5 little prisons. They could eat caviar on Monday and crusts on Tuesday they wouldn't even notice. They know the meaning of the Matrix,
the way the West was won.

They are mobile like the wind,
they belong to the nations,
they need no passport.
People write their addresses in pencil and wonder at their strange existence.
They are free
yet they are slaves
of the hurting and dirty and dying.

What is the vision? The vision is holiness that hurts the eyes.
It makes children laugh and adults angry.
It gave up the game of minimum integrity long ago to reach for the stars.
It scorns the good and strains for the best.
It is dangerously pure.

Light flickers
from every secret motive,
every private conversation.
It loves people away from their suicide leaps, their Satan games.

This is an army
that would lay down its life for the cause.
A million times a day
its soldiers choose to lose that they might one day win the great
"Well done" of faithful sons and daughters.

Such heroes are as radical
on Monday morning as Sunday night.

They don't need fame from names.
Instead they grin quietly upwards
and hear the crowds chanting again and

again:
"COME ON!"
And this is the sound of the underground, the whisper of history in the making, foundations shaking, revolutionaries dreaming once again.
Mystery is scheming in whispers, conspiracy is breathing ... This is the sound of the underground

And the army is discipl(in)ed—
young people who beat their bodies into submission. Every soldier would take a bullet for his comrade at arms.
The tattoo on their back boasts
"for me to live is Christ and to die is gain."

Sacrifice fuels the fire
of victory in their upward eyes.
Winners.
Martyrs.
Who can stop them? Can hormones hold them back? Can failure succeed?
Can fear scare them or death kill them?

And the generation prays
like a dying man with groans beyond talking, with warrior cries,
sulphuric tears and
great barrow loads of laughter!

Waiting.
Watching:
24-7-365.

Whatever it takes they will give:
Breaking the rules,
shaking mediocrity from its cozy little hide,
laying down their rights and their precious little wrongs,
laughing at labels,
fasting essentials.
The advertisers cannot mold them.
Hollywood cannot hold them.
Peer-pressure is powerless
to shake their resolve
at late-night parties
before the cockerel cries.

They are incredibly cool,
dangerously attractive (on the inside).
On the outside? They hardly care!
They wear clothes like costumes:
to communicate and celebrate
but never to hide.

Would they surrender their image or their popularity? They would lay down their very lives, swap seats with the man on death row, guilty as hell:

a throne for an electric chair.

With blood and sweat and many tears, with sleepless nights and fruitless days,
they pray as if it all depends on God and live as if it all depends on them.

Their DNA chooses Jesus
(He breathes out, they breathe in).
Their subconscious sings.
They had a blood transfusion with Jesus.

Their words make demons scream
in shopping malls. Don't you hear them coming?

Herald the weirdoes!
Summon the losers and the freaks.
Here come the frightened and forgotten
with fire in their eyes!
They walk tall and trees applaud, skyscrapers bow,
mountains are dwarfed
by these children of another dimension.

Their prayers summon the Hound of Heaven and invoke the ancient dream of Eden.

And this vision will be.
It will come to pass;
it will come easily;
it will come soon.

How do I know?
Because this is the longing of creation itself, the groaning of the Spirit,
the very dream of God.

My tomorrow is His today.
My distant hope is His 3-D.
And my feeble,
whispered,
faithless prayer
invokes a thunderous,
resounding,
bone-shaking
great "Amen!"
from countless angels,
from heroes of the faith,
from Christ Himself.

And He is the original dreamer,
the ultimate winner.
Guaranteed.

And He is the original dreamer, the ultimate winner. Guaranteed.

DAVID JAMES

LOCATION: BRADFORD, U.K.

BIO: ANGLICAN BISHOP OF BRADFORD

"WE WHO ARE WEAK AND FRAGILE YEARN FOR GOD'S FUTURE, HIS PROMISE IN JESUS FULFILLED, AND OUR PRAYERS, UNFORMED AND TIMOROUSLY WHISPERED, ARE GIVEN MEANING AND SHAPE AND AFFIRMATION FROM OUT OF THE FUTURE BY CHRIST IN GLORY AND THE HOST OF HEAVEN."

My tomorrow is His today.
My distant hope is His 3-D.
And my feeble,
whispered,
faithless prayer
invokes a thunderous,
resounding,
bone-shaking
great "Amen!"
from countless angels,
from heroes of the faith,
from Christ Himself.

How do I know?
Because this is the longing of creation itself,
the groaning of the Spirit,
the very dream of God.

AND THIS VISION WILL BE.
IT WILL COME TO PASS;
IT WILL COME EASILY;
IT WILL COME SOON.

THEIR PRAYERS SUMMON THE HOUND OF HEAVEN
AND INVOKE THE ANCIENT DREAM OF EDEN.

the WEIRDOS!

Summon THE LOSERS and FREAKS,
COME THE Frightened! & FORGOTTEN
with FIRE in their EYES!

THEY WALK TALL and Trees APPLAUD,
Skyscrapers Bow, mountains are dwarfed by these children of another dimension.

JEZ HIGHAM

BIO: TELEVISION DIRECTOR

LOCATION: LONDON, U.K.

"BEFORE I WAS A CHRISTIAN, I TENDED TO HANG OUT WITH 'COOL' PEOPLE. NOW I KNOW SOME 'LOSERS AND FREAKS.' THEY SHOW ME A VERY NEW WAY OF SEEING THINGS AND HELP ME TO RECOGNIZE AND LOVE THE 'LOSER AND FREAK' IN MYSELF."

the vision

BLOOD OF CHRIST
100% PROOF
TYPE "A"

With blood and sweat and many tears,
with sleepless nights and fruitless days,
they pray as if it all depends on God
and live as if it all depends on them.

Their DNA chooses Jesus
(He breathes out, they breathe in).
Their subconscious sings.
They had a blood transfusion with Jesus.

Their words make demons scream
in shopping malls.
Don't you hear them coming?

the Vision

BLOOD OF CHRIST
100% PROOF
TYPE "O"

9780972927628   51399

REACTION
THE VISION & THE

TIM MORRIS-SMITH

LOCATION: SYDNEY, AUSTRALIA

BIO: GENERAL MANAGER & CHARTERED ACCOUNTANT

"I LOVE THESE LINES, AS THEY REMIND ME OF THE POWERFUL TRUTH OF THE GOSPEL THAT IS FLOWING THROUGH MY VEINS, MY HEART, MY BEING, AND SETTING ME FREE."

WOULD THEY SURRENDER THEIR IMAGE OR THEIR POPULARITY?
THEY WOULD LAY DOWN THEIR VERY LIVES,
SWAP SEATS WITH THE MAN ON DEATH ROW, GUILTY AS HELL:
A THRONE FOR AN ELECTRIC CHAIR.

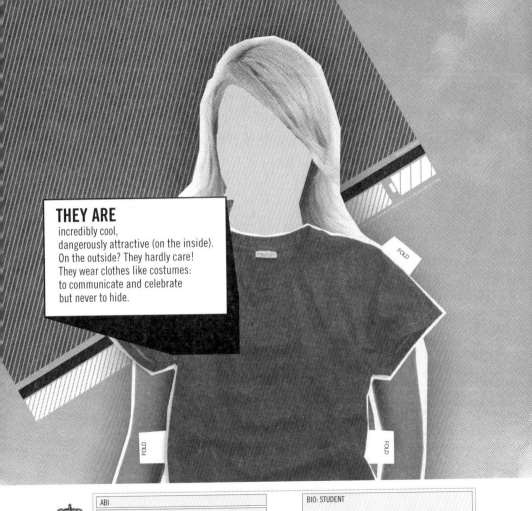

THEY ARE
incredibly cool,
dangerously attractive (on the inside).
On the outside? They hardly care!
They wear clothes like costumes:
to communicate and celebrate
but never to hide.

FOLD

FOLD

FOLD

ABI

BIO: STUDENT

LOCATION: BIRMINGHAM, U.K.

"IN A GENERATION WHERE IMAGE MEANS EVERYTHING, MY CLOTHES ARE JUST A MEANS TO AN END—GETTING ME ACCEPTED BY A GROUP WHO NEEDS DESPERATELY TO KNOW OF JESUS CHRIST."

WHATEVER IT TAKES THEY WILL GIVE:
BREAKING THE RULES,
SHAKING MEDIOCRITY FROM ITS COZY
LITTLE HIDE,
LAYING DOWN THEIR RIGHTS AND THEIR
PRECIOUS LITTLE WRONGS,
LAUGHING AT LABELS,
FASTING ESSENTIALS.
THE ADVERTISERS CANNOT MOLD THEM.
HOLLYWOOD CANNOT HOLD THEM.
PEER-PRESSURE IS POWERLESS
TO SHAKE THEIR RESOLVE
AT LATE-NIGHT PARTIES
BEFORE THE COCKEREL CRIES.

MICHAEL SCHMIDT

LOCATION: COLOGNE, GERMANY

BIO: DESIGNER

"BEING A DESIGNER MYSELF, I REALLY ENJOY THE FACT WE CAN USE THE MEDIA TO COMMUNICATE, ILLUSTRATE, AND NARRATE GOD'S VALUES IN POP CULTURE. LET'S START A MEDIA REVOLUTION!"

And the generation prays
like a dying man
with groans beyond talking,
with warrior cries
sulphuric tears and
great barrow loads of laughter

Sacrifice fuels the fire
of victory in their upward eyes.
Winners.
Martyrs.
Who can stop them?
Can hormones hold them back?
Can failure succeed?
Can fear scare them or death kill them?

REACTION
THE VISION & THE VOW

TOMMIE NAUMANN

LOCATION: THESSALONICA, GREECE

BIO: CHURCH PLANTING PIONEER

"IN A TIME GETTING MORE AND MORE LIKE THAT PREDICTED BY THE PASSIONATE ONE, WITH LOVE COOLING OFF BY THE DAY, THE HEAVENS RESOUND WITH A CLEAR VOICE EMPHASIZING TRUTHS OF OLD … WATCHMAN TAKE YOUR STAND, WAIT AND SEE THIS VISION COME TO FULL MATERIALIZATION. WHAT AN AWESOME DREAM."

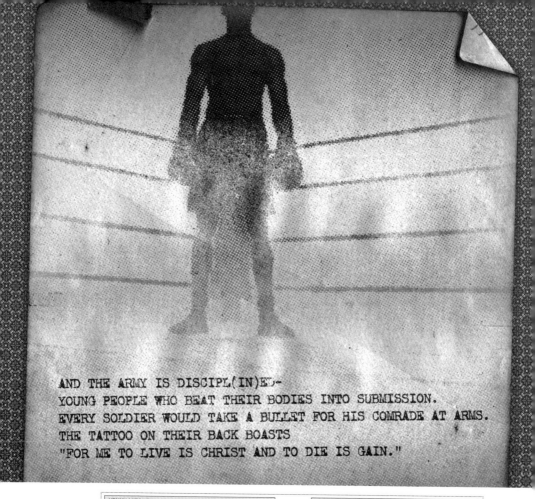

AND THE ARMY IS DISCIPL(IN)ED-
YOUNG PEOPLE WHO BEAT THEIR BODIES INTO SUBMISSION.
EVERY SOLDIER WOULD TAKE A BULLET FOR HIS COMRADE AT ARMS.
THE TATTOO ON THEIR BACK BOASTS
"FOR ME TO LIVE IS CHRIST AND TO DIE IS GAIN."

KENNY MITCHELL

LOCATION: NEW YORK CITY, NEW YORK

BIO: DJ

"LIKE THE SAMURAI OF ANCIENT JAPAN, THIS YOUNG ARMY IS TRAINED IN THE ART OF SERVICE. THIS DISCIPLINED YOUNG ARMY IS DEDICATED AND DEVOTED TO THE SERVICE OF THEIR GOD, THEIR KING, THEIR MAIN MAN JESUS."

AND THIS IS THE SOUND OF THE
UNDERGROUND
THE WHISPER OF HISTORY IN THE MAKING
FOUNDATIONS SHAKING
REVOLUTIONARIES DREAMING ONCE AGAIN
MYSTERY IS SCHEMING IN WHISPERS,
CONSPIRACY IS BREATHING ...
THIS IS THE SOUND OF THE
UNDERGROUND

REACTION
THE VISION & THE VOW

PAUL MERGARD	BIO: SALVATION ARMY MISSION TEAM LEADER
LOCATION: SLACKS CREEK, AUSTRALIA	

"'THE VISION' IS INCREDIBLY PROPHETIC—IT IS HAPPENING RIGHT BEFORE OUR EYES ... IN YEARS TO COME, I'M SURE WE WILL LOOK BACK AND SEE THAT THE UNDERGROUND REALLY HAS RISEN AND NATIONS HAVE BEEN CHANGED."

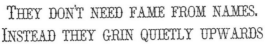

THEY DON'T NEED FAME FROM NAMES.
INSTEAD THEY GRIN QUIETLY UPWARDS
AND HEAR THE CROWDS CHANTING AGAIN AND AGAIN:
"COME ON!"

REACTION
THE VISION & THE VOW

SUSIE FINNEY

LOCATION: SEATTLE, WASHINGTON

BIO: GRAPHIC DESIGNER

"THE FACELESS AND THE NAMELESS ARE AMONG US. WE MAY NOT SEE MUCH OF WHAT GOD IS DOING FOR A WHILE AS THE ANONYMOUS LABOR AND THE WORLD RESTS COMFORTABLE, BUT GOD KNOWS OUR NAMES. AND HE CARES."

Such heroes are as radical on Monday morning as Sunday night.

REACTION
THE VISION & THE VISION

PAUL BRADBURY	BIO: SOCIAL WORKER
LOCATION: PORTSMOUTH, U.K.	

"SUNDAY IS OFTEN WHEN I GET ENVISIONED, BUT MONDAY IS WHEN THE VISION BECOMES A REALITY IN MY WORK WITH SUBSTANCE MISUSERS."

THIS IS AN
MONEY
ARMY
MINE TOO

...aking
low, if
other, it
splurge
making
an there's
tat can sock
ingdom come
ang on, till the
very last dime
ears a hole in the
tl

and I'm fight-
R. But you
vithout

UP. Till that fat pay envelope can't
buy you a square meal.
Stop spending. For yourself. Your
kids. And mine. That, brother, is
sense. Not sacrifice.
Know what I'd do with that dough
... if I'd the luck to have it?
I'd buy War Bonds—and, God,
would I hang on to them! (Bonds
buy guns and give you four bucks
for your three!) . . . I'd pay back
that insurance loan from when Mol-
lie had the baby . . . I'd pony up for
taxes cheerfully (knowing they're
the cheapest way to pay for this war)
I'd sock some in the savings
le I could . . . I'd lift a load
ith more life insurance.
y a shoelace
in the

(You get to knowin'—o
what you can do without

I wouldn't try to profit
war—and I wouldn't ac
anything I had to sell-
all in this together.

I've got your fu
hand, brother. Bu
of ours, in the in
up envelope. Y
guys that a
Street shop

Squeez
got bloo

Use i
make

| KIM HUGHES | BIO: URBAN MONASTIC |
| LOCATION: CALGARY, CANADA | |

"CAN YOU IMAGINE HOW INCREDIBLE IT WILL BE TO HEAR GOD SAY, 'WELL DONE!'? DESPITE ALL THE THINGS I AM SIDETRACKED BY, MY DREAMS OF THAT MOMENT SURPASS MY DESIRE FOR ANYTHING ELSE."

THIS IS AN ARMY

THAT WOULD LAY DOWN ITS
LIFE FOR THE CAUSE.
A MILLION TIMES A DAY
ITS SOLDIERS CHOOSE TO LOSE
THAT THEY MIGHT ONE DAY WIN THE GREAT
"WELL DONE" OF FAITHFUL SONS AND DAUGHTERS.

LIGHT FLICKERS FROM EVERY SECRET MOTIVE, EVERY PRIVATE CONVERSATION. **IT LOVES PEOPLE** AWAY FROM THEIR SUICIDE LEAPS, THEIR SATAN GAMES.

WHAT IS THE VISION

THE VISION IS HOLINESS THAT HURTS THE EYES.
IT MAKES CHILDREN LAUGH AND ADULTS ANGRY.
IT GAVE UP THE GAME OF MINIMUM INTEGRITY
LONG AGO TO REACH FOR THE STARS.
IT SCORNS THE GOOD AND STRAINS FOR THE BEST
IT IS DANGEROUSLY PURE.

| MICHAELA RYALL | BIO: SINGER-SONGWRITER |
| LOCATION: CHICHESTER, U.K. | |

"EVEN WHEN THINGS GET REALLY GOOD, AND I COULDN'T SEE ANY WAY MY LIFE COULD BE BETTER—EVEN WHEN MY RELATIONSHIP WITH GOD IS GREAT—THERE IS ALWAYS MORE."

THEY ARE MOBILE LIKE THE WIND,
THEY BELONG TO THE NATIONS.
THEY NEED NO PASSPORT.
PEOPLE WRITE THEIR ADDRESSES IN PENCIL
AND WONDER AT THEIR STRANGE EXISTENCE.
THEY ARE FREE
YET THEY ARE SLAVES
OF THE HURTING AND DIRTY AND DYING.

REACTION
THE VISION & THE VOW

MARCUS LIND

LOCATION: OREBRO, SWEDEN

BIO: 24-7 BASE LEADER

"IT'S NOT THAT COMMON FOR PEOPLE MY AGE TO HAVE SO MANY WONDERFUL FRIENDS SPREAD OUT AROUND THE GLOBE—WITH THE SAME KIND OF FRUSTRATIONS AND HOPES AND LONGINGS IN THEIR HEARTS."

AND THEY ARE FREE FROM MATERIALISM
THEY LAUGH AT 9-5 LITTLE PRISONS.
THEY COULD EAT CAVIAR ON MONDAY AND CRUSTS ON TUESDAY
THEY WOULDN'T EVEN NOTICE.
THEY KNOW THE MEANING OF THE MATRIX,
THE WAY THE WEST WAS WON.

REACTION

BRENNAN MANNING

LOCATION: NEW ORLEANS, LOUISIANA

BIO: AUTHOR, THE RAGAMUFFIN GOSPEL

"THIS IS MY FAVORITE LINE BECAUSE THE TRIUMPH OF THE HOLY SPIRIT IN A CHRISTIAN'S LIFE IS FREEDOM FROM THE BONDAGE OF MONEY, SEX, POWER, SELF-CONSCIOUSNESS, AND THE TYRANNY OF THE APPROVAL AND DISAPPROVAL OF OTHERS."

THE VISION IS AN **ARMY** OF YOUNG PEOPLE. *you see bones?* I SEE AN **ARMY.**

REACTION
THE VISION & THE YORK

KENNY MITCHELL

LOCATION: NEW YORK CITY, NEW YORK

BIO: DJ

"WE'RE IN THE MIDDLE OF A VISIBLE AND INVISIBLE BATTLE. WE WIELD DIFFERENT WEAPONS—INFUSED WITH ABILITIES OF THE SPIRIT FOR ONE PURPOSE AND ONE PURPOSE ONLY—THE CAUSE OF THE KINGDOM."

THE VISION?
the vision is jesus
OBSESSIVELY
dangerously
undeniabiy
jesus

REACTION
THE VISION & THE VOW

| TRE SHEPPARD | | BIO: LEAD SINGER, ONE HUNDRED HOURS |
| LOCATION: U.K. | | |

"THIS LINE STRIKES ME EVERY SINGLE TIME I HEAR IT ... JESUS IS THE VISION. HE HAS ALWAYS BEEN THE REAL REVOLUTIONARY IN A SEA OF IMITATORS."

"Write this. Write what you see.
Write it out in big block letters so
that it can be read on the run. This vision-message
is a witness pointing to what's coming. It aches for the
coming—it can hardly wait! And it doesn't lie. If it seems slow
in coming, wait. It's on its way. It will come right on time.
Look at that man, bloated by self-importance—full
of himself but soul-empty. But the person in
right standing before God through loyal
and steady believing is fully alive, really alive."
(Habakkuk 2:2-4 MSG)

Vision" all those nights ago was the beginning of a journey that continues to this day. This book attempts to take you on that journey with me, along the road that leads from "The Vision" to *The Vow*.

My prayer is that through these pages, you would come closer to Jesus in every way. He is, after all, the one who sums up *The Vision* and *The Vow* in word, in life, in death, and even in us for His glory. What grace! C'mon!

Pete Greig
(Chichester, U.K./Kansas City, U.S.A.)

before God, and who cast themselves on his mercy. Startled by the extravagant love of God, they do not require success, fame, wealth, or power to validate their worth. Their spirit transcends all distinctions between the powerful and powerless, educated and illiterate, billionaires and bag ladies, high-tech geeks and low-tech nerds, males and females, the circus and the sanctuary."[3]

Wherever I go, I find such people, such communities, enjoying God while immersing themselves shamelessly in His world. Seeking to pray like it all depends on God and to live like it all depends on them. Trying to give Jesus "Access All Areas." Painfully aware of their own stupidity and the genius of grace. Passionate about Jesus and therefore in love with His world. Holy against the odds.

A pretty girl with an explosion of bleached hair was addressing the congregation: "As it says in 'The Vision,'" she said, as if "The Vision" was a book in the Bible with which everyone present should be entirely familiar, "As it says in 'The Vision,'" she repeated, "'For me to live is Christ, and to die is gain.'" She finished speaking with the solemnity of a bishop presiding at a funeral, and I screamed "Noooooooo!" (silently in my head of course). "Those words are from the BIBLE," I wanted to yell, "I merely plagiarized the Apostle Paul!"

At that moment, I realized that it might be a good idea to provide some kind of context to my prayer-poem-thing—to offer a biblical framework that might help people surf the underlying themes to some deeper place of timeless truth in the Word of God.

So that's where this book was born. In the next few pages, you will find the original words of "The Vision" illustrated and illuminated, as were ancient Celtic manuscripts, but with the symbols of our time. Access the book from the other side, and you will find *The Vow*, fifteen chapters exploring some of the greatest themes of scripture: grace, discipleship, and covenant. For me, the writing of "The

This invisible network is perhaps more a shared longing than a structural reality. It would be easy (and lazy) to define this emerging community in negatives: tags like non-religious, postmodern, post-evangelical, or non-hierarchical; such terms have all been given plenty of airtime already. But actually, as I analyze the various strands of thought in the emerging Christian worldview, I see something very positive: They all share a single longing—to practice a life-affirming, grace-inspired spirituality that combines true intimacy with God with active and unapologetic involvement in society. Intimacy and involvement. Both together.

Of course, in theory, most Christians advocate being "in the world and not of it." But in practice, so many of our predecessors and peers seem to have actually adopted one of these poles at the expense of the other. As a result, they have ended up either intimate but irrelevant or involved but impotent through compromise.

Thus there is a legitimate sense of urgency about this call to influence through intimacy and involvement—enjoying God in worship, holiness, and an alternative worldview, while truly engaging actively and joyfully with the hopes and hurts of the big, bad world.

I guess "The Vision" has spread because it simply expresses what so many people are already seeking to live. If you're flowing with this movement, you will feel the connection powerfully as you read these words. But if you're not, you will probably wonder what all the fuss is about!

We are envisioned, but we are not superheroes. Quite the reverse. Our intimacy with God is the gift of grace, not the attainment of piety. Our involvement in society is inspired by mercy, not militancy. Grace is the heartbeat of our vision. As usual, Brennan Manning puts it far better than I ever could, describing this movement, this "ragamuffin rabble," as "the unsung assembly of saved sinners who are little in their own sight, conscious of their brokenness and powerlessness

3. Brennan Manning, *Ruthless Trust* (SPCK, London: 2000) p. xiii.

five-hundred-seat tent with just twelve people trying to pray for a campus mission he didn't really believe in, he became extremely depressed: "I hid in a dark corner and wept uncontrollably feeling unwanted, unloved, and useless," he recalled. Eventually he crept over to the stereo and, with the headphones on, found himself listening to a track that "described everything I ever wanted in my life." He listened to "The Vision" six times back-to-back that night: "For the first time," he explained, "Christianity was being described in a way that resonated perfectly with my search …"

As such stories filtered back to me, I was left shaking my head, again and again, in total amazement. From China to Columbine, and from Basque teenagers to British directors, these late-night words scribbled in a private moment on a prayer room wall had somehow taken on a life of their own and were now mysteriously touching lives all round the world.

ℭONSPIRACY THEORY

The question I've often asked myself is, "Why?" And as I've traveled and talked to a lot of people, the theory I've formulated is this: I think "The Vision" has spread because it resonates with a much bigger thing that God is doing in our time. These words seem somehow to have given voice to an undercurrent, some kind of contemporary spiritual coalition that is neither organized nor an organization and doesn't have a name (thank God!). There isn't one single website to bookmark, no brand bigging itself up, no T-shirt to wear, no single gathering point (there are thousands).

But one of the clues that such a movement may well be stirring is the way that, every now and then, there comes along a song, a sermon, a story, a movie, or even a poem like mine, that just seems to touch a nerve because it spreads unexpectedly all over the world.

- Meanwhile, DJs in New York, Sweden, England, and Wales got a hold of a rough recording of me reading the words and did their own remixes, adding samples, beats, and even movie clips.

- On a train to London one day, a television filmmaker listened to one of these mixes and began physically trembling with the impact right there in the carriage. "I never knew I could believe anything so passionately," he said.

One of the most moving stories came to my attention when the Columbine High School shootings were still fresh in the minds of a reeling America, and seventeen-year-old Rachel Joy Scott had recently been recognized as a modern day martyr (she was explicitly singled out and shot dead for her faith). Her uncle, John Phillips, suddenly found his life turned upside-down by grief, but also by invitations to visit schools across America to tell his niece's remarkable story. Shell-shocked and grieving, he gathered a bunch of national leaders seeking their blessing upon his growing ministry. Standing before them, apparently lost for words, he pulled some crumpled papers from his pocket: "I found these words on the Internet," he stammered. "And they're the only way I can convey to you what God is doing in our schools right now ..." He began to read "The Vision," pausing on lines that were particularly poignant:

"Every soldier would take a bullet ...

'For me to live is Christ, to die is gain ...'"

As John Phillips stood before those dignitaries reading these words in remembrance of his martyred niece, he wept.[2]

Another moving story came from a newly converted student struggling with his sexual orientation and acute depression. Late one night, finding himself in a

---

2. Recounted to me by Bob Jobe at the Contra Corriente festival, Spain. For more on this and many other stories associated with "The Vision," see *Red Moon Rising* by Pete Greig and Dave Roberts (Relevant Books), chapter 11.

have seemed strange, they said it encouraged them to see that God is moving in Western youth culture in answer to their prayers!

- Meanwhile, as "The Vision" secretly circulated Communist China, it was being used rather more publicly in Washington, D.C. at a gathering of hundreds of thousands in the Capitol Mall for The Call—first of many such mass prayer gatherings around the world. Believers on different continents, persevering under different ideologies, united in their vision of Christ.

- A fifteen year old from Bilbao, Spain, was so impacted by "The Vision" that he kick-started a movement called La Resistencia, which has since grown into one of the most exciting youth ministries in the Basque region, uniting churches, enduring its fair share of persecution, and leading young people to Jesus in one of the hardest mission fields in Europe.

As my piece of innocent graffiti began to hitch-hike it's way around the world, it also catalyzed surprising creativity along the way:

- An American dance group choreographed "The Vision" and performed the piece in front of a thousand people in Valladolid, Spain.[1]
- An art student in England spent many weeks turning the words into elaborate graffiti on a four-meter panel for her dissertation piece. The university must have been impressed: "The Vision" now hangs like writing on the wall in the campus canteen.

1. *www.contracorriente.org*

asleep in bed?

So I begin to write my "why" on the wall. And as I do so, a stream of ideas (which had been fidgeting around in my head for years) just sort of tumble onto the paper. I leave my poem on the wall amidst a load of other prayers and go home to bed.

I still don't really know how or why it happened, but those words got a pulse. Somehow they just walked out of the room. The first thing I knew about it was an email from a guy in Canada: "Hi, Pete, I came across this poem-thing on the Internet and thought you'd like it …" Clicking the link, I found myself reading my own words, which had been beamed to me seven thousand miles from the room downstairs.

The following month, friends gathered at an event called Cultural Shift in Southampton, U.K., seeking to explore the meaning of church in the emerging culture. It was Sunday morning, and several hundred of us had hired out a local nightclub for a time of worship. I read out my prayer-room rant with DJ Andy Hunter mixing in some big beats, and the place went crazy—people yelling "c'mon!" like it was some kind of war-cry. Something seemed to be stirring—the words were invoking a latent passion in the crowd.

No one really knew where "The Vision" (as it was nicknamed) had come from, and, to be honest, it didn't really matter. In a way, we'd all written it together in a thousand different conversations, spoken and silent. I just used the pen.

But before long, "The Vision" was connecting powerfully with people all over the world:

- It was translated into Mandarin and published in an underground newspaper read by more than a million persecuted Chinese believers. Although some of the cultural reference points must

It's the middle of the night,
and I'm in a room trashed with prayer.
Childish graffiti spiders the walls.
CDs lie scattered on the carpet tiles.
Moldy coffee cups.
Painting stuff.
Beats on the stereo.
A candle.
A globe.
Red Bull.

No wonder it's trashed. For weeks we've been here, praying like never before. Back-to-back, in one-hour shifts, right through the days and these long winter nights.

And I'm trying to work out why.

When did I turn into a certified weirdo?

What am I doing here, at three o'clock in the morning, trying to talk to God (whose very existence many of my friends doubt) when normal people are all

THE VISION

THE VISION ...

is a poem, a prayer, a prophecy (in part). A surf trip, a pit stop, a new pair of shades, and an old pair of shoes. 722 words. Sight for sore eyes. Some kind of catwalk for God's new clothes. Too much coffee. A diary. A dowry. Déjà vu. Stream of consciousness, sound-bite snack. A life-sentence. A telescope in a microscope. A mirror on the wall. Dust breathing. A body waking from a long sleep, blinking, stretching: "What shall we do today?" Disjointed. Mercury falling. Connecting flight. Red moon rising. Thousand-year heart. A bucket ...

AND ...

A spade. A mustard seed for Jack. A snapshot for tourists, for pilgrims a sound track. A video. A voyage. A big fat bass amp making me dance. A meeting place. Writing on the wall. Heart-graffiti. My own private twister. A smile in a fist. A fist in a fight. The fight of my life. An answer in search of a question. A meditation, invocation, declaration of intent. Terms of engagement, call to arms. A conversation with culture and scripture and Christ. A movement wondering, a worldview wishing, a dreaming of life. Rhythm and blues of

... THE VOW

For all of us …
"The days are near when every vision will be fulfilled."
(Ezekiel 12:23)

°the Vision

°the Vow and
A CALL TO DISCIPLESHIP

PETE GREIG

[RELEVANTBOOKS]

"Your young men will see visions."
(The prophet Joel)

"The Vision" has touched literally millions of lives already, having spread by word of mouth from a single room in England to Washington D.C., Sydney, Australia, and the underground Church of China. These words, written by Pete Greig, have stirred artists, DJs, filmmakers, and countless ordinary people to live "dangerously, obsessively, and undeniably" for Jesus.

This inspiring book is the only published account of "The Vision." Broken down line-by-line and fully illustrated, "The Vision" in this book will resonate with the vision in your heart that longs to rise up and live beautifully, love passionately, and give everything to impact the culture. Flip the book, and you can begin a journey from "The Vision" to *The Vow*—a voyage of discovery that really could change your life forever.

[RELEVANTBOOKS]
WWW.RELEVANTBOOKS.COM